CW00665274

"With insight and inspira[t]
McLaughlin shows us the
ness, majesty, compassion, [a]
wonderful reading."

—*SAM ALLBERRY*, pastor and author

"Rather than view women as risks, liabilities, or burdens, Jesus invites them to draw near. With her characteristic and refreshing blend of scholarship and empathy, Rebecca McLaughlin invites us to examine the stories of women woven throughout the ministry of Jesus, searching for the common threads of good news. And a clear, unhesitating message emerges: 'Suffer the women to come unto me.' Herein is instruction and encouragement for women and men alike seeking to live as brothers and sisters in God's family."

—*JEN WILKIN*, author and Bible teacher

"In this mind-stimulating and soul-stirring book, Rebecca McLaughlin reveals that far from dismissing and devaluing women, early Christianity was countercultural for the common good. Indeed, it was propelled by women who were truly known and deeply loved. As we look through the eyes and lives of women in the Gospels, we can more clearly see Jesus in all of his resolute truth and radiant beauty."

—*JULIUS J. KIM*, president, The Gospel Coalition

Published by The Gospel Coalition

The Gospel Coalition
P.O. Box 170346
Austin, Texas 78717

Art Direction: Brannon McAllister and Gabriel Reyes-Ordeix
Cover Design: Lindy Martin, Faceout Studio
Typesetting: Ryan Leichty

ISBN:
978-1-956593-07-5 (paperback)
978-1-956593-06-8 (ebook)
978-1-956593-08-2 (kindle)

Printed in the United States of America

JESUS
THROUGH
THE EYES
OF WOMEN

How the First Female Disciples
Help Us Know *and* Love the Lord

REBECCA McLAUGHLIN

CONTENTS

For Grace,
who will see Jesus soon.

INTRODUCTION

IN 1896, in an antiquities market in Cairo, a manuscript dealer sold an ancient papyrus. The buyer was a German scholar named Carl Reinhardt. The dealer told Reinhardt that a peasant had found the book in the niche of a wall. But this romantic story is unlikely to be true. The papyrus dates from the fifth century and was so well-preserved that it cannot have spent 1,500 years in the open air. When Reinhardt examined the manuscript, he found that it contained four previously unknown ancient texts, including a partial copy of a book that has come to be known as the Gospel of Mary.

Two other fragments of the Gospel of Mary have been discovered since, and experts believe that it was originally written in the second century. Substantial sections of the text in each copy are missing. But what remains relates a meeting between Jesus and his disciples after his resurrection. One disciple, Mary, has received special revelation from Jesus. But when Mary shares what Jesus has disclosed to her, Peter accuses her of lying.

He does not believe that Jesus has given this revelation to a woman. Mary weeps at the charge.

Mary's experience resonates with countless women throughout the last 2,000 years who have been dismissed and devalued by their brothers in Christ. In fact, some see Christianity as, at heart, misogynistic: silencing, sidelining, and trampling on women. At the academic, all-girls high school I attended and afterward at Cambridge University, I had many conversations with women and men who thought that women's rights are antithetical to Christianity—or at least to any form of Christianity that clings to the Bible as its source of truth. I now live in Cambridge, Massachusetts. But the perception of Christianity among many of my peers remains the same: the chrysalis of Christianity must be shed for the butterfly of women's rights to fly.

For some scholars, the Gospel of Mary and other so-called Gnostic Gospels offer Christianity a life raft when it comes to women. In fact, some have suggested that early church leaders suppressed a more female-oriented version of Christianity that texts like the Gospel of Mary preserve. But in this book, I want to argue that, far from suppressing women's voices and devaluing their lives, the first-century Gospels of Matthew, Mark, Luke, and John connect us to the testimony of the women who met Jesus in the flesh 2,000 years ago, and that the Jesus we see through their eyes is more beautiful, more historically accurate, and more valuing of women than anything the Gospel of Mary can offer.

JESUS'S EFFECT ON WOMEN

The four New Testament Gospels tell multiple stories of Jesus relating to women. Poor women. Rich women. Sick women. Grieving women. Old women. Young girls. Jewish women. Gentile women. Women known for their sinfulness. Women known for their virtue. Virgins and widows. Prostitutes and prophetesses. Looking through their eyes, we see a man who valued women of all kinds—especially those vilified by others. Indeed, the way that Jesus treated women tore up the belief that women are innately inferior to men: a belief that was pervasive in the ancient world. We should not be surprised, therefore, that women have been flocking to Jesus ever since.

In its first few centuries, Christianity was known for its attractiveness to women and to slaves. The Roman governor Pliny the Younger wrote to the emperor Trajan in the early second century, asking for advice on how to handle Christians. To find out more about the strange new faith infecting his region, Pliny had tortured "two female slaves, who were called deaconesses." This biopsy of the church was representative of its members. While women and slaves were dispossessed in Greco-Roman culture, they could hold meaningful leadership positions in the church, like these two enslaved women who were recognized as deaconesses. When the late second-century Greek philosopher, Celsus, quipped that Christians "want and are able to convince only the foolish, dishonorable and stupid, only slaves, women, and little children," he was painting a caricature, but one grounded in truth.[1] In fact, from the earliest evidence we have about the composition of the church to our best data today, it seems that Jesus has always been more attractive to women than to men.

Records of one North African church that was raided during the Great Persecution—which lasted from AD 303 to 313—document the seizure of disproportionately female clothing: 13 pairs of men's shoes versus 47 pairs of women's; 16 men's tunics versus 82 women's; and 38 women's headdresses.[2] Likely, this clothing was intended for the poor. But even among wealthy Christians, women seem to have outnumbered men. In the period before the conversion of the Roman emperor Constantine in 337, we have the names of 40 Christians of the senatorial class. Two-thirds of them were women.[3] So, why were women drawn to Christianity?

In *The Triumph of Christianity: How a Forbidden Religion Swept the World*, New Testament scholar and skeptic Bart Ehrman explains that, while the Roman empire was extremely diverse, its inhabitants shared some basic assumptions. "If one word could encapsulate the common social, political, and personal ethic of the time," Ehrman writes, "it would be 'dominance.'" He goes on:

1. See Michael J. Kruger, *Christianity at the Crossroads: How the Second Century Shaped the Future of the Church* (Downers Grove, IL: IVP Academic, 2018), 34–35.

2. See Helen Rhee, *Loving the Poor, Saving the Rich: Wealth, Poverty, and Early Christian Formation* (Grand Rapids, MI: Baker Academic, 2012), 154.

3. See Peter Lampe, *From Paul to Valentinus: Christians at Rome in the First Two Centuries* (Minneapolis: Fortress Press, 2003), 119.

In a culture of dominance, those with power are expected to assert their will over those who are weak. Rulers are to dominate their subjects, patrons their clients, masters their slaves, men their women.[4]

But Christianity upended this belief. As Ehrman puts it,

Leaders of the Christian church preached and urged an ethic of love and service. One person was not more important than another. All were on the same footing before God: the master was no more significant than the slave, the patron than the client, the husband than the wife, the powerful than the weak, or the robust than the diseased.[5]

This ethical reversal, based on Jesus's words and actions, made Christianity especially attractive to women in the ancient world and formed the basis of our modern belief that women are fundamentally equal to men. Far from being antithetical to women's rights, Christianity is their first and best foundation.

In the last two millennia, Christianity has gone from being the faith of a tiny minority to the most widespread and racially and culturally diverse belief system in the world. And Jesus's magnetic effect on women is undiminished. A 2015 report found that across the world, 33.7

4. Bart Ehrman, *The Triumph of Christianity: How a Forbidden Religion Swept the World* (New York: Simon & Schuster, 2018), 5.
5. Ehrman, *Triumph of Christianity*, 5–6.

percent of adult women identify as Christians versus 29.9 percent of men, and the disproportion is likely growing. The church in China is one of the fastest growing Christian movements in the world—on track to have more Christians than the United States within five years—and it's disproportionately female. What's more, Christian women globally are significantly more likely than men to attend church weekly[6] and pray daily.[7] They're also more likely than men to read the Bible for themselves—even if it takes substantial effort.[8] A few years ago, a Chinese friend told me that after her illiterate grandmother became a believer, she began stopping people in her apartment block and pleading with them to help her read just a couple verses of her Bible. But is all this embrace of Christianity doing women any good? Or is Jesus like a terrible boyfriend women just can't seem to leave, despite the harm?

6. An analysis of 53 countries found that 53 percent of self-identified Christian women said they attended church at least once a week, versus 46 percent of Christian men. See "The Gender Gap in Religion Around the World," Pew Research Center, March 22, 2016, https://www. pewforum.org/2016/03/22/women-more-likely-than-men-to-affiliate-with-a-religion/.

7. Across 54 countries analyzed, 61 percent of Christian women report praying daily compared to 51 percent of Christian men. See "The Gender Gap in Religion Around the World," https://www.pewforum. org/2016/03/22/women-report-praying-daily-at-higher-rates-than-men/.

8. The 2020 State of the Bible survey, commissioned by the American Bible Society, found that "women are more Scripture engaged than men." It reports that more than half of American women (52 percent) are "Bible friendly," "Bible engaged," or "Bible centered," compared to 47 percent of American men.

Far from being bad for women, being actively religious (which, for most in the West, includes regular church attendance) seems to come with more happiness and better mental health. For example, a large-scale study published by scholars at the Harvard School of Public Health in 2016 found that U.S. women who attended religious services at least once a week were five times less likely to kill themselves than those who never attended.[9] Likewise, a study published in 2020 found that U.S. women who attended religious services weekly were 68 percent less likely to die deaths due to suicide, drug overdose, or alcohol than those who never attended, while men who attended weekly were 33 percent less likely to die such deaths.[10] Strikingly in the United States, more than one-third of actively religious adults (36 percent) describe themselves as "very happy," compared with just a quarter (25 percent) of both inactively religious (e.g., those who identify as Christians but do not go to church) and religiously unaffiliated Americans.[11]

9. Tyler J. VanderWeele et al., "Association Between Religious Service Attendance and Lower Suicide Rates Among US Women," *JAMA Psychiatry* 73, no. 8 (2016), https://jamanetwork.com/journals/jamapsychiatry/article-abstract/2529152.

10. Ying Chen et al., "Religious Service Attendance and Deaths Related to Drugs, Alcohol, and Suicide Among US Health Care Professionals," *JAMA Psychiatry* 77, no. 7 (2020), https://jamanetwork.com/journals/jamapsychiatry/article-abstract/2765488?mc_cid=469f806293&mc_eid=796e84b78.

11. See, "Religion's Relationship to Happiness, Civic Engagement and Health Around the World," Pew Research Center, January 31, 2019, https://www.pewforum.org/2019/01/31/religions-relationship-to-happiness-civic-engagement-and-health-around-the-world/.

What's more, while the biblical limitation of sex to lifelong marriage has often been billed as an unhealthy straightjacket—refusing women (and men) the sexual freedom thought to be the path to happiness—the data points in the opposite direction. A growing body of evidence has shown that, for women especially, having multiple sexual partners is correlated with lower levels of mental health and happiness.[12] Conversely, far from being locked into misery, the happiest wives in America are highly religious women married to highly religious men.[13] Couples who pray together, read Scripture at home, attend church, and so on are twice as likely as their secular peers to say they are satisfied with their sexual relationship.[14] We might think that Christian marriage is robbing women of sexual freedom. But the data suggests

12. See, for example, Tyree Oredein and Cristine Delnevo, "The Relationship between Multiple Sexual Partners and Mental Health in Adolescent Females," *Journal of Community Medicine & Health Education* 3, no. 7 (December 2013), which found that "the prevalence of sadness, suicide ideation, suicide plans and suicide attempts increased with the number of sexual partners across all racial/ethnic groups"; and Sandhya Ramrakha et al., "The Relationship between Multiple Sex Partners and Anxiety, Depression, and Substance Dependence Disorders: A Cohort Study," *Archives of Sexual Behavior* 42, no. 5 (February, 2013), https://www.ncbi.nlm.nih.gov/pmc/articles/PMC3752789, which found "a strong association between number of sex partners and later substance disorder, especially for women."

13. See W. Bradford Wilcox, Jason S. Carroll, and Laurie DeRose, "Religious Men Can Be Devoted Dads, Too," *New York Times*, May 18, 2019, https://www.nytimes.com/2019/05/18/opinion/sunday/happy-marriages.html.

14. Matthew Saxey and Hal Boyd, "Do 'Church Ladies' Really Have Better Sex Lives?," Institute for Family Studies, November 16, 2020, https://ifstudies.org/blog/do-church-ladies-really-have-better-sex-lives.

that it's pulling women (and men) away from the train wreck of commitment-free sex.

Does this mean Christianity is only for virgins and happily married mothers of four? No. As we meet Jesus in the Gospels, we'll encounter a man who welcomes sexually notorious women while standing up to sexually self-righteous men. We find a man born into sexual scandal, who further scandalized his fellow Jews by loving women known for sexual sin. We find a man who never had a sexual relationship, but who loved women so well that they'd leave everything to follow him. We find a man who turned his back on the religiously powerful men of his day and had his longest recorded private conversation with a religiously despised woman. Throughout this book, we'll look at Jesus through these women's eyes. But can we have any confidence that what we read about Jesus in his four New Testament biographies is accurate and that texts like the Gospel of Mary don't offer us a more authentic view?

CAN WE TRUST THE GOSPELS?

In his groundbreaking book *Jesus and the Eyewitnesses*, British New Testament scholar Richard Bauckham argues convincingly that the texts of Matthew, Mark, Luke, and John are not the products of generations of oral tradition—as many 20th-century scholars assumed—but that they preserve for us eyewitness testimony from people who knew Jesus personally. This book will draw extensively on Bauckham's work, including his outstanding

Gospel Women, and will argue that the testimony of women in particular is vital to the story that the Gospel authors tell.[15]

Mark's Gospel is generally recognized as the first to be written, likely between 35 and 45 years after the events it records. Bauckham observes that this dating is "well within the lifetime of many of the eyewitnesses," and he argues that Matthew, Luke, and John "were written in the period when living eyewitnesses were becoming scarce, exactly at the point in time when their testimony would perish with them were it not put in writing."[16] By comparing the way names are used in the Gospels with how eyewitnesses are cited in other texts from the same period, Bauckham makes a compelling case that the Gospel authors are pointing their readers to their sources for the stories that they tell. But could eyewitnesses really remember these events so long after they occurred?

I'm not old enough to remember things that happened 35 to 45 years ago—let alone 60 years, which is the likely gap between when the author of John spent time with Jesus and when he wrote his Gospel down. If you're younger than 50, those time frames probably sound impossibly long. We forget most of what happened to us

---

15. Richard Bauckham, *Jesus and the Eyewitnesses: The Gospels as Eyewitness Testimony* (Grand Rapids, MI: Wm. B. Eerdmans, 2006); Bauckham, *Gospel Women: Studies of the Named Women in the Gospels* (Grand Rapids, MI: Wm. B. Eerdmans, 2002). A second edition of *Jesus and the Eyewitnesses* was published in 2017, though I will be quoting from the first edition.

16. Bauckham, *Jesus and the Eyewitnesses*, 7.

last week! But my parents, who are in their 60s, and my grandparents, who are in their 80s, easily recall the most important events and conversations from their teens and 20s—especially those they've told and retold to their children and grandchildren and great-grandchildren. My grandpa, for example, remembers the day when my mother as a small child insisted that she wanted to walk to school alone. My grandpa let her go but followed at a distance. It turned out, she had planned to meet up with a boy who had been bullying her little sister for a fight! This happened almost 60 years ago, and even though it wasn't a life-changing event, it stuck in grandpa's mind, and he's told the story with amusement down the decades. Jesus's disciples devoted themselves to watching what he did and learning what he taught. This was a full-time job, not just for Jesus's 12 chosen apostles but also for the dozens of people (including many women) who traveled with Jesus. After Jesus's death and resurrection, they went from place to place proclaiming what they'd heard and seen. When the Gospel authors came to write accounts of Jesus's life, they had a wealth of testimony to draw from—not least, the testimony of Jesus's female disciples.

What about the other so-called Gospels, like the Gospel of Mary? While the four New Testament Gospels were all written within the lifetimes of eyewitnesses to Jesus's life, the Gospel of Mary is believed to have been written in the early- to mid-second century—well after the eyewitnesses died out.[17] Rather than being rooted in the Old Testament, the Gospel of Mary, like other so-called Gnostic Gospels, depends much more on Greek philosophy than Hebrew Scripture and assumes a different view of the world, in which matter is evil and salvation involves escape from the physical. This is fundamentally different from the Judeo-Christian belief in the goodness of God's original creation, and the Christian promise of embodied, resurrection life for all who trust in Jesus. Unlike the Gospels in our Bibles, the Gospel of Mary does not give us an account of Jesus's earthly life. It's purely focused on supposed conversations after Jesus's resurrection. If we had this text and not the texts of the Gospels in our Bibles, we would know almost nothing about the life, death, and resurrection of Jesus of Nazareth, and we would have only a tiny proportion of his recorded teachings—teachings that have changed the world.

We might think the Gospel of Mary was suppressed because it makes Peter look bad. Peter, after all, was a key leader in the early church. But rather than airbrushing the mistakes of Jesus's male disciples, the Gospels in our Bibles—including the Gospel of Mark, which is thought to be based on Peter's testimony—frequently paint the apostles (and Peter in particular) in a terrible light. For example, all four Gospels record that Peter denied even knowing Jesus three times on the night Jesus was arrested.

17. See Karen L. King, *The Gospel of Mary of Magdala: Jesus and the First Woman Apostle* (Santa Rosa, CA: Polebridge Press, 2003), 3.

By contrast, the women among Jesus's disciples are noted for their faithfulness, and each of the Gospel authors depends on the testimony of women at vital points in their accounts. In fact, if we worked through the Gospels in our Bibles and cut all the scenes *not* witnessed by women, we would only lose a small portion of the texts. If we cut the things that *only* women witnessed, we'd lose our first glimpse of Jesus as he took on human flesh and our first glimpse of his resurrected body. The four Gospels preserve the eyewitness testimony of women. The central question of this book is, "What did Jesus look like through their eyes?"

WOMEN IN THIS BOOK

When my 3-year-old son Luke has done something he's proud of, he asks me, "Mommy, did you get a glimpse of me?" His phrasing is both preschool awkward and profound. Even as his mother, I'll only ever really get a glimpse of him. His father, sisters, teachers, and friends all see him from different angles, and like snapshots used to make a 3D image, we could compile them to get a better sense of who he is. Still, we'd only get a glimpse of him. When it comes to Jesus, this reality is multiplied. We cannot hope to capture him. But according to the Gospels, he has come to capture us: not to deprive us of our rights and lock us up, but to restore us to our rightful habitat with him.

From the first moments of his life on earth, Jesus was gazed upon by women. In this book, we will examine the stories of these women and see what Jesus looked like through their eyes.

Chapter 1 will look at Jesus through the lens of prophecy, focusing on the testimony of Jesus's mother, Mary, her elderly cousin, Elizabeth, and a prophetess named Anna, who prophesied over Jesus when he was brought to the temple as an infant. We will see how these women were given prophetic words from God to show us both who Jesus is and also what he would do.

In chapter 2, we'll see that many of Jesus's disciples were women—some traveling with him, others staying where they were. We'll see what we can learn from the named women among Jesus's itinerant disciples. Then we'll focus on two of Jesus's closest female friends, Mary and Martha of Bethany.

The theme of chapter 3 is nourishment. We'll witness Jesus's first miracle in the Gospel of John, when at his mother's request he turned gallons of water into the finest wine. We'll listen in on his longest recorded private conversation, which was with a Samaritan woman at a well, to whom he offered living water. We'll see both the epic fail and the redemption of the mother of two of Jesus's apostles, and we'll look at a shocking conversation between Jesus and a Syrophoenician woman who recognized that Jesus is the source of real bread.

Chapter 4 will trace a line through Jesus's healings of women: from Simon Peter's feverish mother-in-law, to a woman who bled for 12 years, to a 12-year-old girl whom Jesus raised from the dead, to a disabled woman he healed on the Sabbath. We'll see how each of these women shines a light on Jesus's identity.

Chapter 5 will focus on forgiveness. We'll see how Jesus welcomed a notoriously sinful woman and held her up as an example of love, and how he protected a woman who had been caught in adultery and used her situation to expose the sin of the religious leaders.

Finally, in chapter 6, we'll see how much the Gospel authors depend on the eyewitness testimony of women when it comes to Jesus's resurrection. The resurrected Son of God was first seen through the eyes of women, and women were the first to be entrusted with his news of life.

The Gospels present Jesus as the one true, living God—the God who made the universe, the God who, according to Scripture, humans cannot see and live. To get a glimpse of Jesus is to risk your very life. But according to Jesus, it's also to find it. Weeping women with their faces to the ground saw Jesus, while certain men stood face-to-face with him and had no idea who they were looking at. We don't need the second-century Gospel of Mary to see who Jesus is. We need the first-century Gospels of Matthew, Mark, Luke, and John, which draw on the eyewitness testimony of women from the beginning.

PROPHECY

THE FIRST PERSON to hear the good news about Jesus was a low-income teenage girl from a Podunk town. She was the first to find out Jesus's name, the first to know he was the Son of God, the first to realize that her son would be God's everlasting, death-defying King. This girl had the most common name of her day—a name belonging to one in five Jewish women of her time and place.[1] She was just another Mary. But then an angel came to her. And in an instant, the backwater world of this small-town girl became the place where God stepped in.

In this chapter, we'll look at Jesus's mother, Mary, and at two other women—Elizabeth and Anna—whom God anointed with the gift of prophecy to recognize Jesus. We'll see how Jesus's birth reached back into history and

---

1. Surviving records indicate that over 20 percent of Jewish women in the region were named Mary. See Richard Bauckham, *The Testimony of the Beloved Disciple: Narrative History and the Theology of John's Gospel* (Grand Rapids, MI: Baker Academic, 2007), 175.

forward into eternity, and we'll get our first intoxicating taste of the role that women played in Jesus's life on earth: from its beginning to its bitter end—and beyond.

PROPHECY AND PREGNANCY

For years, I kept the test that first told me I was pregnant. Two pink lines announced that in nine months, my baby would be born. I looked and felt no different. But this small piece of plastic proclaimed the extraordinary truth: I was a mother. Miranda is 11 now and full of random questions. Last week, she asked me if I'd like to be able to see the future. I replied, "No way!" The weight of that knowledge would hang on me like a constricting snake. But did I want to know, all those years ago, that she was growing in my womb? Yes. Absolutely.

In the Old Testament, prophecy functions a little bit like a pregnancy test. It speaks the truth about the present and the future—however dissonant the two might seem. Like a pregnancy test in the hands of hopeful parents, prophecy can bring glad tidings of great joy or devastating news of loss, and God's people had experienced both. Centuries before Jesus was born, prophets warned that his judgment would come if they did not repent. God's people didn't listen. So, the northern kingdom of Israel fell to the Assyrians. Then, after more prophetic warnings, the southern kingdom of Judah was conquered by the Babylonians. In the midst of this, the prophets promised that one day God would send an everlasting King to rescue his people—a king even better than Israel's greatest king,

David. For instance, living as an exile in Babylon, Daniel had a vision of someone "like a son of man, coming with the clouds of heaven," who received from God himself "dominion and glory and a kingdom, that all peoples, nations, and languages should serve him . . . an everlasting dominion, which shall not pass away" (Dan. 7:13–14). But, like parents longing year after year for a child and never getting pregnant, God's people waited and waited and no such King had been born.

When the Persians took control from the Babylonians, things started to look up. The Jews returned to their land and rebuilt their temple, but they were still living under foreign, pagan rule. The Persians were succeeded by the Greeks, and God's people lived under a succession of local Greek dynasties that advocated the spread of Greek culture and religion. Eventually, the Jews were barred from practicing their faith, and the temple in Jerusalem was turned into a pagan shrine. This was an utter low point for God's people. But devastation spurred revolt, and finally the Jews became self-governing again. In 164 BC, the temple was cleansed, and daily offerings resumed—a moment Jews still celebrate today at Hanukkah. This seemed like a fresh start. For the first time in centuries, God's people were no longer living under pagan rule, and for 100 years, one family reigned. Perhaps God's promises were coming true at last! But still there was no everlasting king, and from the second generation onward, there was significant internal strife.

Strikingly, the last monarch in this dynasty to hold the throne successfully was a woman: Queen Salome

Alexandra. Her husband, King Alexander Jannaeus, bequeathed her the throne when he died, and she ruled from 75 to 67 BC. The years Queen Salome Alexandra reigned were ones of prosperity and renewed religious observance. But after her death, one of her sons seized the throne from his older brother. The civil war that ensued only ended in 63 BC, when the Roman general Pompey took Jerusalem and desecrated the temple. God's people were crushed under foreign, pagan rule once more.

Things could have been worse. The Jews were allowed to worship as they wanted, and in 37 BC, the Romans appointed an official king of the Jews, Herod the Great, who undertook a major renovation of the temple. But Herod was not ethnically Jewish himself, and he was only a puppet king, ruling under Roman authority. Any attempt to resist imperial power was stamped out like a cigarette butt. This was the weary world in which a Jewish girl named Mary was born.

We don't know much about Mary's background, except that she was relatively poor, that she was engaged to a man named Joseph, and that she lived in a backwater village in Galilee called Nazareth. So far so unimpressive. But Mary of Nazareth was the woman to whom God sent an angel with the prophecy that God's ancient promises were coming true at last.

The angel Gabriel began: "Greetings, O favored one, the Lord is with you" (Luke 1:28). Mary knew she was no one special, but here was an angel saying the opposite, and she was "greatly troubled" (Luke 1:29). Gabriel went on:

Do not be afraid, Mary, for you have found favor with God. And behold, you will conceive in your womb and bear a son, and you shall call his name Jesus. He will be great and will be called the Son of the Most High. And the Lord God will give to him the throne of his father David, and he will reign over the house of Jacob forever, and of his kingdom there will be no end. (Luke 1:30–33)

The prophet Isaiah had spoken of a king who would be born to sit on David's throne forever (Isa. 9:6–7). Micah had spoken of a ruler who would be born in David's hometown of Bethlehem, who would bring peace to the ends of the earth (Mic. 5:2–5). The angel Gabriel's news, delivered to one small-town teenage girl, was like a flaming torch unleashed in the darkness, a song of hope amid the groans of Jewish pain. It was a call to arms with a promise of unquestionable victory. God's long-awaited King was on his way. His name would be Jesus, which means "the Lord saves," and he would be Mary's son.

SON OF GOD

Doubtless reeling from Gabriel's words, Mary had a practical question: "How will this be, since I am a virgin?" (Luke 1:34). Perhaps she thought her fiancé, Joseph, would be the father. But Gabriel drops another bomb:

The Holy Spirit will come upon you, and the power of the Most High will overshadow you; therefore the child to be born will be called holy—the Son of God. (Luke 1:35)

Even regular conception feels miraculous. I remember staring at the lines on the pregnancy test and pondering the inconceivable: a whole new human life had quivered into being in my womb. When I first felt Miranda kick, I kept fixating on the fact that she was someone else— and yet within me. It was truly unbelievable. But Mary's experience was something else. The angel said that the Holy Spirit of God—the Spirit who hovered over the nothingness before creation, the Spirit who inspired great kings and prophets—would overshadow her, and then the Son of God himself would grow and stretch and kick within her womb.

We're so accustomed to the claim that Jesus is the Son of God that it's hard for us to wrap our minds around how wild this message was. Stories were told of Greek and Roman deities impregnating human women. But the God of the Old Testament was not remotely like these pagan gods. He was utterly transcendent, the one true maker of all things, the one whom humans could not see and live, the God who, when asked for his name, replied, "I AM WHO I AM" (Ex. 3:14). To be sure, God's prophets had painted the promised, everlasting King in more-than-human terms. But that he'd be the *literal* Son of God would've been shocking to first-century Jewish ears. Mary could have been ostracized, or even stoned to death, for getting pregnant outside marriage. Saying, "Don't worry, the baby's father is the great I AM himself" would only have added blasphemy charges to her account. Yet Mary responded at once with obedient faith: "Behold, I am the servant of the Lord; let it be to me according to your word" (Luke 1:38).

RECEIVING JESUS

How do we see Jesus through Mary's eyes at this moment? We see him as the everlasting Son of God, the promised King, the great "I AM" made flesh. Through Mary's eyes, we also see the life-upending blessing of receiving Jesus, and how he can only be received by those who know they're nothing more than servants of the Lord. Of course, we cannot stand in Mary's shoes. You and I have not been called to be the mother of God's only Son. She carried in her womb the one through whom all wombs were made. She nursed the one who generated life on earth. She reared the one who formed the stars. But as we look at Jesus through his mother's eyes, we see how God grabs ordinary folk to be his chosen agents in this world. When you and I let Jesus in, our humdrum lives become the buzzing center of a miracle—however little it may feel that way at times.

Last Christmas, my daughter Eliza asked for a watch that tracks your steps, like one I have. As December progressed, she kept reminding me to buy the watch. I'd purchased it already, but I was noncommittal, hoping that she'd be a little bit surprised on Christmas Day. When Eliza unwrapped her gift, she was thrilled: it was exactly what she asked for! But when she opened the box, it was empty. I accidently wrapped the empty box of the watch I bought myself a few months earlier. Eliza thought I pranked her. Perhaps that's how you feel today. You're trying to believe God loves you and to trust his promises, but life right now life feels like an unwrapped giftbox with no contents. Perhaps you're wondering if God is there, or if he really cares for you at all. But just as it must have seemed quite inconceivable to Mary that God's promises from centuries before were coming true in her, if we're pinning our hopes on Jesus, however empty you or I might feel today, the truth is that we're unimaginably full of life and love.

From the moment of Jesus's conception, Mary's life was paradoxical: she had become the mother of the one through whom all things were made (John 1:3). And if we put our trust in Jesus now, our lives become a paradox as well: we are the body here on earth of him who made our bodies and our earth. We are his hands and feet and arms and mouth.

As we look through Mary's eyes, we also see the cost of letting Jesus in. Birth itself is intensely costly. Nursing an infant day and night is an ongoing act of sacrificial love. Amid the joy of meeting my first child, I cried repeatedly in the first days and weeks of Miranda's life. Everything hurt. I couldn't sleep. I worried desperately about her, fearing she'd go to sleep and never wake, while also longing for her times of sleep. I felt like I had lost my life by gaining hers. I loved her, and she ruined me. For Mary, two millennia ago, every risk was multiplied—the risk of her own death in childbirth or that her son would die in infancy. But Mary risked much more with Jesus than she would have with another child. She risked her reputation, her marriage prospects, her community, even her life when she replied to Gabriel, "Behold, I am the servant of the Lord: let it be to me according to your word" (Luke 1:38).

It seems from Luke and Matthew's accounts that Mary didn't tell her fiancé she was pregnant with God's Son. Joseph heard about it later, from an angel (Matt. 1:18–21). But after Gabriel left her, Mary rushed to see the one person who might understand: her older relative, Elizabeth, who lived down south, some 80 to 100 miles away.

ELIZABETH

Elizabeth and her husband, Zechariah, are the first two people we meet in Luke's Gospel. Zechariah was a priest, and Elizabeth was "from the daughters of Aaron"—in other words, from the priestly family. Luke tells us that "they were both righteous before God, walking blamelessly in all the commandments and statutes of the Lord. But they had no child, because Elizabeth was barren, and both were advanced in years" (Luke 1:5–7). Chronic infertility can be profoundly painful. My friends who have experienced it report the many feelings it can surface, and in particular, how hard it is to witness others all around them having kids while they become increasingly hopeless. The lack of children would've felt yet more disastrous to Zechariah and Elizabeth, in a culture where infertility came with shame, especially for the would-be mother. But six months before he appeared to the teenage girl in Nazareth, Gabriel appeared to Zechariah while he was serving in the temple and told him that Elizabeth would have a son named John, who would be "filled with the Holy Spirit, even from his mother's womb" (vv. 13–15). By the time Gabriel visited Mary, Elizabeth was six months pregnant. Gabriel's last words to Mary were these: "your relative Elizabeth in her old age has also conceived a son, and this is the sixth month with her who was called barren. For nothing will be impossible with God" (vv. 36–37).

The first story in Luke is Gabriel's meeting with Zechariah, which might make us think that God would fulfill his ancient promises through Zechariah and Elizabeth's son. After all, the story of the Jews began with a promise to an old and childless man named Abraham and his wife Sarah (Gen. 12:2–3). But instead of Zechariah stepping into Abraham's sandals, it's Mary whose son will be the Promised One. When Abraham's son Isaac was born, the future of all God's people was embodied in his infant form. When Mary gave birth to Jesus, he embodied all God's people too. Jesus is the Chosen One in whom God's self, God's people, and God's promises converge. But Zechariah and Elizabeth's baby, later known as John the Baptist, played a vital role as well. Jesus identified John with the great Old Testament prophet Elijah, sent to prepare the way for the promised Messiah (Matt. 11:14). Before John was old enough to speak a word and Zechariah still unable to speak, however, Elizabeth spoke prophetic words to Mary.

Luke could've easily cut this scene between Mary and Elizabeth without disrupting the narrative. But he gives space for us to hear prophetic words from both these women—words that have echoed through the centuries—because Mary and Elizabeth are not *only* the biological mothers of Jesus and John. They also act as prophetesses in their own right. When it comes to women's unique ability to bear children, it's easy to make one of two mistakes: to overvalue childbearing, as if it's the primary reason why women exist, or to undervalue it, as if creating new life doesn't matter. The full-orbed picture Luke gives us of these two pregnant women helps us not to fall into either trap.

When Mary arrives at Elizabeth's house, her voice sets off a chain reaction. First, the unborn baby John leaps in Elizabeth's womb. Then Elizabeth is "filled with the Holy Spirit" (Luke 1:41). In the Old Testament, great leaders of God's people or great prophets were at times filled with the Spirit (e.g., Num. 27:18; Ezek. 2:2; Mic. 3:8). Later in the story, Zechariah will be "filled with the Holy Spirit" and will prophesy (Luke 1:67). But here Elizabeth is Spirit-filled, and God reveals to her who Jesus is. On hearing Mary's greeting, she cries out,

> Blessed are you among women, and blessed is the fruit of your womb! And why is it granted to me that the mother of my Lord should come to me? For behold, when the sound of your greeting came to my ears, the baby in my womb leaped for joy. And blessed is she who believed that there would be a

fulfillment of what was spoken to her from the Lord. (Luke 1:42–45)

Mary doesn't need to tell Elizabeth her news. Elizabeth knows. The Holy Spirit has revealed to her what Mary had been told by Gabriel. She knows that Mary is carrying her Lord, and that Mary believed what God promised her. At times in the Old Testament, God spoke through female prophets.[2] Here, God grants Elizabeth the gift of prophecy to glimpse who Jesus is, even before he is born. Chronologically, these are the first prophetic words spoken by a human and recorded in the Bible since the prophet Malachi four centuries earlier.

As a much older, married woman, Elizabeth is Mary's social superior. But Jesus changes everything. This is Elizabeth's moment of glory. The cultural shame of her infertility is removed. She's pregnant with a prophet, she's filled by the Holy Spirit, and what does she say? Words that humble her and exalt her younger relative. As we look through Elizabeth's eyes, we see that Jesus is our Lord, even when that's not remotely how things seem. Jesus is in embryonic form, invisible to human eyes. He has no earthly power at all. But Spirit-filled Elizabeth knows better. She knows she's in the presence of her Lord.

2. For example, Deborah (Judg. 4:4) and Huldah (2 Kings 22:14–20; 2 Chron. 34:22–28).

PRAISING GOD

Up to this point in Luke's Gospel, Mary has only had two lines. Luke is holding back so that her next speech hits like a tornado. Responding to Elizabeth's prophetic outburst, Mary delivers one of the longest and most powerful speeches made by anyone in the Gospels besides Jesus himself:

> My soul magnifies the Lord,
>> and my spirit rejoices in God my Savior,
> for he has looked on the humble estate of his servant.
>> For behold, from now on all generations will call me blessed;

> for he who is mighty has done great things for me,
>> and holy is his name.
> And his mercy is for those who fear him
>> from generation to generation.
> He has shown strength with his arm;
>> he has scattered the proud in the thoughts of their hearts;
> he has brought down the mighty from their thrones
>> and exalted those of humble estate;
> he has filled the hungry with good things,
>> and the rich he has sent away empty.
> He has helped his servant Israel,
>> in remembrance of his mercy,
> as he spoke to our fathers,

to Abraham and to his offspring forever.
(Luke 1:46–55)

Mary sees where she stands in the great sweep of God's promises from Abraham onward. She recognizes the extraordinary privilege she has and how all generations will call her blessed. But rather than focusing on herself, Mary pours herself out in praise to God. Her speech is like a gorgeous tapestry woven from many Old Testament threads. But, in particular, her words echo the speech of an Old Testament mother who delivers one of the most magnificent speeches made by any human being in Scripture.

Like Elizabeth, Hannah was chronically infertile. But she prayed to God for a child, and he gave her a son who became the prophet Samuel. Hannah's prayer of thanksgiving for Samuel's birth begins like Mary's: "My heart exults in the LORD" (1 Sam. 2:1). Like Mary, Hannah goes on to praise the God of great reversals: "The bows of the mighty are broken, but the feeble bind on strength. Those who were full have hired themselves out of bread, but whose who were hungry have ceased to hunger. . . . [The LORD] raises up the poor from the dust; he lifts the needy from the ash heap to make them sit with princes" (1 Sam. 2:4–5, 8a; Luke 1:51–53). But even more significantly, Hannah's speech ends with a direct prophecy about the Christ, God's promised King: "The LORD will judge the ends of the earth," Hannah concludes, "he will give strength to his king and exalt the horn of his anointed" (1 Sam. 2:10). The word translated "his anointed" here is the first time the Hebrew Scriptures uses the word from which we get "Messiah" in a direct prophecy about God's King. Our English word "Christ" is from the Greek form of this word. Hannah's prophecy reached its first fulfillment when her son, Samuel, anointed Israel's first two kings, Saul and David. But the ultimate fulfillment of Hannah's prophecy is Jesus himself.

Hannah is the first to prophesy directly about the Lord's anointed King. Mary is the first to find out his identity. Looking at Jesus through the ancient telescope of Hannah's and Mary's eyes, we see the one who turns the tables on all human power, the one who lifts the humble and humbles the mighty, the one who is the Savior of his people, showing mercy even as he shows his strength.

BIRTH

I've given birth three times. With every comfort of a modern hospital, complete with epidural, it was still an agonizing and undignified experience. The pain, blood, and exposure involved in bringing a new human into this world is inescapable—however many yoga balls and meditation practices you use. But giving birth in poverty 2,000 years ago was something else. There was a significant risk of death in childbirth, and Mary does it far from home and without the most basic comforts. Jesus is born in Bethlehem: the birthplace of King David. But far from being born in royal luxury, he comes into the world in poverty. Famously, Mary "wrapped him in swaddling cloths and laid him in a manger, because there was no place for them in the inn" (Luke 2:7). Mary prophesies that, through Jesus, the Lord would exalt the poor at the expense of the rich (1:52–53). When she lays Jesus in an improvised crib, she witnesses the pivot point of this reversal, as the greatest king in history was wrapped up in her poverty.

Jesus's poor birth is not an accident. It is a sign. That night, an angel appears to local shepherds, who themselves are poor and low-class. The angel says to them,

> Fear not, for behold, I bring you good news of great joy that will be for all the people. For unto you is born this day in the city of David a Savior, who is Christ the Lord. And this will be a sign for you: you will find a baby wrapped in swaddling cloths and lying in a manger. (2:10–12)

Jesus's birth is good news of great joy for all the people. But it's this band of ragtag shepherds who receive divine notification—not the religious or political leaders. When the shepherds find "Mary and Joseph, and the baby, lying in a manger" they pass the angel's message on to anyone who will listen (vv. 16–18). But Luke highlights Mary's response especially: "Mary treasured up all these things, pondering them in her heart" (v. 19). How do we see Jesus through Mary's eyes at this moment? We see him as the one through whom God's promises are already coming true. We see that the lack of room at the inn is not a mistake, but a message. Jesus came for the poor and excluded first. But he is also a Savior for all the people: rich and poor, male and female, young and old. As Mary learns to nurse her son, she also learns more of who he really is: "a Savior, who is Christ the Lord" (v. 11).

SACRIFICE AND SWORD

One of the side effects of birth is weeks of bleeding. It's not glamorous. The Old Testament law prescribed a period of time for a mother's postpartum bleeding to stop before she brought her infant to the temple in Jerusalem. When Mary and Joseph take the month-old Jesus to the temple to make the sacrifice required for a firstborn, their poverty is underscored again as they offer the lower-income sacrifice: "a pair of turtledoves, or two young pigeons" (Luke 2:24). But poverty can't hide who Jesus is. Luke tells us that a man named Simeon "came in the Spirit into the temple," took Jesus in his arms, and blessed God (vv. 27–28). He'd been told that he wouldn't die before he saw "the Lord's Christ" (v. 26), and now that moment had come. But after praising God, and blessing both Mary and Joseph, Simeon says these troubling words to Mary in particular: "Behold, this child is appointed for the fall and rising of many in Israel, and for a sign that is opposed (and a sword will pierce through your own soul also), so that the thoughts of many hearts may be revealed" (vv. 34–35).

Gabriel told Mary she was highly favored of God. Elizabeth told her she was blessed among women. But Simeon's words must have cut her to the core. A sword would pierce her soul? Mary had already risked disgrace.

She'd already experienced the pain of childbirth and its demanding aftermath. But this most blessed of women has more suffering to come. If we look at Jesus through Mary's eyes in this moment, we see that being close to Jesus means embracing suffering. As she listens to Simeon, Mary gets a glimpse of the future. Jesus would be opposed, and her heart would be impaled. But even as she's taking in these words, God sends a prophetess to reassure her.

ANNA, THE PROPHETESS

I've called this chapter "Prophecy" and maybe you've been thinking it's a stretch to use that term for words from Mary's and Elizabeth's mouths. But as Luke concludes his narrative of the events around Jesus's birth, he introduces us to a woman whom he directly calls a prophetess:

> And there was a prophetess, Anna, the daughter of Phanuel, of the tribe of Asher. She was advanced in years, having lived with her husband seven years from when she was a virgin, and then as a widow until she was eighty-four. She did not depart from the temple, worshipping with fasting and prayer day and night. And coming up at that very hour she began to give thanks to God and to speak of him to all who were waiting for the redemption of Jerusalem. (Luke 2:36–38)

Anna's name—which in Hebrew is Hannah—is one she shares with only one other person in the Bible: the mother of Samuel. The name was quite uncommon at the time, so the connection would have jumped out to first-century Jews.[3] Like Hannah, Anna is known for her unrelenting prayer. Hannah prophesied about the Messiah, through whom the Lord would judge the ends of the earth, and Anna comes to prophesy over the Messiah, who has been born at last. Anna ties the threads on the tapestry Mary had woven from Hannah's words.

Anna is an elderly widow—the kind of woman who is all too often ignored in our culture today. She's been single for the vast majority of her life, and she's completely devoted to the Lord: worshiping and praying day and night. The level of detail Luke gives us on her background is remarkable. Luke tells us Anna's father's name and that she comes "from the tribe of Asher" (v. 36). The original territory of Anna's tribe was in the western hills of Galilee. But the tribe of Asher was all but wiped out in the judgment on the northern kingdom of Israel. Anna appears here as a remnant of that tribe, reuniting the two historic kingdoms of Israel and Judah as a Jerusalem-based prophetess from a devastated northern tribe. Anna has also witnessed an impressive swath of Jewish history. At 84, she was born at a time when the Jews were self-governing, lived through the prosperous

3.   Richard Bauckham notes, "Of the 247 Jewish women in Palestine from the period 330 BC–200 CE whose names are known, our Anna is the only one who bears this name." Bauckham, *Gospel Women*, 92.

reign of Queen Salome Alexandra, and saw the crushing end of Jewish sovereignty when the Romans took over in 63 BC.

Anna, the aged widow, looks very different from Mary, the teenage mother. They represent two ends of a timeline as they each gaze on Jesus. But both women receive revelation from the Lord about the promised King through whom God would at last redeem his people. On seeing Jesus, Anna "began to give thanks to God and to speak of [Jesus] to all who were waiting for the redemption of Jerusalem" (v. 38). Mary and Elizabeth prophesied in private. Anna prophesies in public: in the temple to all who are waiting for God's rescue. Through her eyes, we see Jesus as the Redeemer of God's people, come not to restore Jewish self-rule, as in the time of Queen Salome Alexandra, but to work a redemption so much greater than political self-government.

Anna is not the first person to prophesy over Jesus. But if we think chronologically, she is the first person in the Bible officially called a prophet since the death of the last Old Testament prophet, Malachi, some four centuries before. Malachi prophesied, "the Lord whom you seek will suddenly come to his temple; and the messenger of the covenant in whom you delight, behold, he is coming, says the LORD of hosts" (Mal. 3:1b). The prophetess Anna now witnesses the coming of the Lord into his temple, as the 1-month-old Jesus is brought there in his mother's arms. But while Anna's words of redemption are comforting, Mary soon experiences the truth of

Simeon's troubling prophecy about the opposition Jesus would face.

MAGI AND MURDER

One of my earliest childhood memories is of my mother taking me to her choir rehearsal in London. I remember the massive concert hall and the stunning voices surrounding me as I sat on the steps, waiting for my mother, and feeling the awe of it all. The refrain of the song I remember them rehearsing begins, "See his star shining bright."

The tune springs across octaves in a dramatic and beautiful way, as if to explain how heaven and earth came together when Jesus was born. The words draw inspiration from Matthew's account of wise men from the east who came to Jerusalem saying, "Where is he who has been born king of the Jews? For we saw his star in the east and have come to worship him" (Matt. 2:1–2).

The coming of the wise men—or magi—likely happens some months after Jesus's birth, and while they are evidently highly educated, their wisdom apparently does not extend to politics. If it did, they might have known to steer well clear of Herod, the current king of the Jews. Herod asks the chief priests and the scribes where the Christ was meant to be born. They answer, "In Bethlehem of Judea" and pointed to a prophecy from Micah (vv. 5–6; Mic. 5:2). So, Herod sends the wise men to Bethlehem, claiming he wants to worship the new King too.

The magi come to Jesus on their knees: "going into the house, they saw the child with Mary his mother, and they fell down and worshiped him. Then, opening their treasures, they offered him gifts, gold and frankincense and myrrh" (Matt. 2:11). For Mary, this visit must feel like confirmation of the things the angel had promised. Her boy is being venerated not by shepherds this time, but by wealthy, highly educated foreigners. However, when they leave, the grim reality of Simeon's warning sets in. In an attempt to eliminate Jesus, Herod orders a slaughter of all boys younger than 2 in Bethlehem, and Mary and Joseph have to flee to Egypt (vv. 13–18). How Mary must have clung to Anna's words as she experiences this threat and time of exile. Yes, Jesus is God's promised King. But from his infancy, she sees how controversial Jesus is. Some travel long and far to worship him, while others hate Jesus so much that they want him dead.

Not long afterward, Herod himself dies. His equally dangerous son assumes the rule of Judea, and Mary and Joseph settle back in Nazareth. But the effects of brutal Roman rule are inescapable. Right after Herod's death, a man named Judas led a rebellion in the region and captured an armory in Sepphoris, a larger town four miles from Nazareth. The Romans responded with decisive force: they burned Sepphoris to the ground, sold its people into slavery, and crucified about 2,000 Jews.[4] This is the world in which Mary raises her son: the son

4. The Jewish historian Josephus reports this in his *Antiquities of the Jews* 17.10.

who's supposed to be God's empire-breaking King. It is a world in which attempts to throw off Rome's control led straight to crucifixion. This most blessed of women will live with this distressing knowledge as she sees her son grow up. Yes, God showed her favor, but a sword would one day pierce this mother's heart.

The vulnerability of motherhood begins with pregnancy. I worried every day of my first pregnancy that it would end and that my baby would be lost. My kids are growing now: 11, 9, and 3. Right now, they're healthy, happy, and—most meaningfully—recognizing Jesus as their Lord. But every day I wrestle with concerns about their future. What if severe depression strikes my kids? What if their hearts are broken or their bodies are irrevocably harmed? What if, most frightening of all to me, they turn away from Jesus in the end? Living as a parent feels like sending out your heart into the world without your body: unprotected, out of your control. How Mary must have felt this fear, knowing who her son was born to be, and getting this first glimpse of how he'd be opposed!

BACK TO THE TEMPLE

The last glimpse we get of Jesus's childhood through Mary's eyes is when he's 12. Mary and Joseph bring him back to the temple for Passover. After the feast, his family leaves. But Jesus doesn't. Mary and Joseph get a whole day's journey out of Jerusalem before they realize Jesus isn't with them. They retrace their steps and scour Jerusalem for three days, their panic doubtless escalating.

Finally, they find Jesus in the temple, sitting among the teachers, listening to and questioning them. Luke tells us that "all who heard him were amazed at [Jesus's] understanding and his answers" (Luke 2:47). But Mary asks him, "Son, why have you treated us so? Behold, your father and I have been searching for you in great distress" (v. 48). Jesus answers, "Why were you looking for me? Did you not know that I must be in my Father's house?" (v. 49). Despite all God's revelations of Jesus, Mary didn't get it. Luke tells us that Mary and Joseph "did not understand the saying that he spoke to them" (v. 50). But once again, Mary "treasured up all these things in her heart" (v. 51).

As I look through Mary's eyes in this moment, I see my own inadequacy. Mary is the first to receive the wonderful news about Jesus. And yet she cannot grasp who Jesus really is, and how much more he would be than all she can imagine. I know that Jesus is the Son of God. But much of the time, I go about my life as if this truth need not disrupt my every moment. I live as if my plans can prosper without Jesus at the heart of them. But Jesus cannot fit around our lives, brought in when he's convenient. He's either Lord of everything we have, and are, and ever will become—or he is not. Like Mary, I can go whole days forgetting Jesus. I can push on with my plans. But then, I have to double back. If I could really see who Jesus is, I'd know each second of my life belongs to him. Like almost all the people close to Jesus in the Gospels, we see the times when Mary fails to recognize who Jesus is. And yet, as we'll explore in chapter 3, we also see how Jesus sticks with her and cares for her until the end.

Mary, Elizabeth, and the prophetess Anna lived very different lives. Mary was young and poor and seemingly insignificant. Elizabeth lived most of her life with the cultural shame and personal grief of infertility. Anna had been widowed young and was now old. But each spoke words inspired by God that help us see who Jesus is. Much of what we know about Jesus's conception, infancy, and childhood we only know because the women who surrounded him passed on their testimony. As we look through their eyes today, may we see Jesus as who he truly is: the Son of God, born in poverty, revealed in history, sent to redeem his people and to be God's promised, everlasting, universal King.

DISCUSSION QUESTIONS

Getting Started: Share about a time when you received exciting news. How did you respond? It could be something big, like finding out you got your dream job, or something simple, like learning the person in front of you at the coffee shop bought your drink.

1. How do the events in Israel's history leading up to Mary's day help us see the significance of Gabriel's announcement in Luke 1:30–33?
2. What do we know about the backgrounds of Mary, Elizabeth, and Anna?

3. Why is it significant that women spoke prophetic words about Jesus?

4. The Bible describes an upside-down kingdom of God that is totally different from what we might expect—the first are last, the lowly are exalted, and the King comes to die. How does the birth of Jesus to Mary fit into this picture of God's kingdom?

5. What do Hannah's, Mary's, and Elizabeth's pregnancies have in common? What do they reveal about God's character?

6. In what ways did Mary experience pain or distress from knowing Jesus? How does her experience relate to the Christian life?

7. How have you struggled with feeling insignificant, overlooked, or outcast? How can the stories of the women in this chapter bring you hope in your discouragement?

8. How do you see Jesus most meaningfully through the eyes of these women?

Going Deeper: Read Hannah's prayer of thanksgiving for Samuel's birth in 1 Samuel 2:1–10 and Mary's prayer in Luke 1:46–55.

1. What similarities do you see between Hannah's prayer and Mary's prayer? What characteristics of God do they praise?

2. What prophecy does Hannah give in 1 Samuel 2:10? How does Mary's prayer signal its fulfillment?

3. Hannah and Mary both emphasize God's strength and mercy. On which of these qualities do you tend to focus? How might holding God's mercy and strength together affect your worship?

DISCIPLESHIP

"WHY DIDN'T JESUS have any women disciples?" My 9-year-old, Eliza, always asks the hardest questions, and they come rapid fire. Quite often, when she starts her inquisition, I begin with "I'm not really sure." Part of my job as a parent is being honest when I don't know. But when she asked *this* question, I just smiled and said, "He did."

In this chapter, we'll meet the named women among Jesus's itinerant disciples. Then we'll focus on two women—Mary and Martha of Bethany—who did not travel with Jesus, but who were nonetheless among his closest followers. As we see Jesus through these women's eyes, we'll see him as a Jewish rabbi like no other: a teacher sent by God to change the world. But we'll also see how impossible it is to say that Jesus is no more than that. In fact, we'll see that claiming that Jesus is *just* a good teacher is like saying the sun is *just* a source of light.

JESUS'S FEMALE DISCIPLES

Eliza had good reason for her question. The 12 tribes of Israel began with the 12 sons of Abraham's grandson Jacob, and Jesus chose 12 Jewish men as his "apostles," signaling a new start for God's people.[1] Mark describes the apostles like this: "he appointed twelve (whom he also named apostles) so that they might be with him and he might send them out to preach and have authority to cast out demons" (Mark 3:14–15). From this point on, when Mark uses the word "disciples," he tends to mean these 12 apostles. But Luke explains that the 12 were a subset of Jesus's disciples. After a night of prayer, Jesus "called his disciples and chose from them twelve, whom he named apostles" (Luke 6:13). So, what about the larger group of disciples who traveled with Jesus? Luke makes it clear that this larger group included many women.

After telling a story of Jesus forgiving a notoriously sinful woman and commending her over a self-consciously religious man, Luke writes:

Soon afterward [Jesus] went on through cities and villages, proclaiming and bringing the good news of the kingdom of God. And the twelve were with him, and also some women who had been healed of evil spirits and infirmities: Mary, called Magdalene, from whom seven demons had gone out, and Joanna, the wife of Chuza, Herod's household manager, and

1. Matt. 19:28 and Luke 22:30 highlight this connection.

Susanna, and many others, who provided for them out of their means. (Luke 8:1–3)

Luke notes that many of the women who traveled with Jesus had been healed by him—whether physically or spiritually—and that his ministry was supported financially by his female followers. This is significant. Luke often focuses our eyes on the poor and marginalized. But here we get a glimpse of the rich women who were drawn to Jesus—so captivated by him that they left their homes and followed him wherever he went. As we saw in the introduction, the Gospel authors named people in order to flag them as eyewitness sources. When Luke names these three women in particular, he is likely signaling that they are among the witnesses on whose testimony he draws for his account of Jesus's life.

Mary Magdalene comes first and has become by far the most famous of Jesus's female disciples. Instead of being distinguished from all the other Marys by reference to a husband or a son, she's identified as coming from her hometown—just as Jesus is sometimes called "Jesus of Nazareth." We don't know this Mary's marital status or whether she had children. We don't know what she looked like or anything about her sexual history. The idea that she was a reformed prostitute was introduced centuries after her death. All Luke tells us is that Jesus cast seven demons out of her. Mary Magdalene had been utterly ravaged by spiritual forces of evil—the last person we might expect to be recruited to the Son of God's core team. But Jesus likes to pick the most unlikely people, and this Mary not only travels with Jesus during his ministry, she also plays a critical role in testifying to Jesus's resurrection. Mary Magdalene went from being a playground of demons to a key player in God's topsy-turvy plan to change the world. How do we glimpse Jesus through her eyes? We see him as the one who utterly transformed her life—the one who lifted her out of a demonic pit and set her on her feet as a devoted disciple.

The second woman Luke names—"Joanna, the wife of Chuza, Herod's household manager"—is far less famous today than Mary Magdalene. You could read Luke's Gospel 10 times and not remember her. But Joanna would have stuck in Luke's first readers' minds because of her status and connection with the man who imprisoned and beheaded John the Baptist. This Herod is not King Herod the Great, who ruled when Jesus was born, but one of his sons, Herod Antipas, who rules over Galilee during Jesus's ministry. Luke tells us that when Herod Antipas hears about Jesus, he wants to meet him: "John I beheaded," he says, "but who is this about whom I hear such things?" (Luke 9:9). How does Luke know about Herod's reaction? Quite likely through Joanna. As Herod's household manager, Chuza would hold a high rank in Herod Antipas's court. His wife would have access to the court gossip, and her abandonment of court comforts to travel with a controversial rabbi would cause a stir.[2]

2. See Bauckham, *Gospel Women*, 136–37.

In fact, Joanna's decision to become a disciple of Jesus is nothing short of dangerous. Herod is intrigued by Jesus, but he also wants to kill him (13:31). After Jesus is arrested, the Roman governor Pilate sends Jesus to Herod, and Luke tells us, "When Herod saw Jesus, he was very glad, for he had long desired to see him, because he had heard about him, and he was hoping to see some sign done by him" (23:8). But Jesus won't answer Herod's questions or put on a show, so "Herod with his soldiers treated [Jesus] with contempt and mocked him" (23:11). As a member of Herod's court, Joanna takes a tremendous risk by leaving everything to follow Jesus, and the unique insights Luke has about Herod's thinking and behavior may well be thanks to her.

Joanna's high social status also makes clear that the women who traveled with Jesus were not included simply to perform domestic tasks. In fact, Bauckham argues that it is "quite mistaken to suppose that the women [in Luke 8:1–3] are assigned, within the community of Jesus's disciples, the kind of gender-specific roles that women played in the ordinary family situation."[3] A woman of Joanna's status would have had servants back home to cook and clean for her. Rather, the wealthy women among Jesus's disciples funded his mission. Of course, this doesn't mean they never got their hands dirty. Jesus taught his followers again and again that serving others is intrinsic to discipleship. He even got down on his knees and washed their feet (John 13:1–17). But Luke's

3. Bauckham, *Gospel Women*, 114.

naming of Joanna, in particular, undermines the idea that the women were brought along to keep house for the men. How do we see Jesus through Joanna's eyes? We see him as the one who chooses people from his enemy's court to serve in his kingdom. We see him as the one for whom all status must be sacrificed, all friends in high places left behind, the one on whom our money should be spent, the one for whom we must risk everything.

The last woman Luke mentions by name he simply calls Susanna. Her name was not common, so she did not need distinguishing. But she must have been well known for Luke to pick her out from the larger group of female disciples. Luke's carefulness in referencing his eyewitness sources is illustrated when he cites Mary Magdalene and Joanna, but not Susanna, as witnesses of Jesus's resurrection. Instead, Luke mentions "Mary the mother of James" (Luke 24:10). Likely Susanna was not among the women who went to Jesus's tomb and found it empty, but Luke had consulted her about earlier episodes in Jesus's life. Just as Luke gives us Mary, Elizabeth, and Anna as witnesses of Jesus as an unborn and a newborn, so now he gives us Mary Magdalene, Joanna, and Susanna as witnesses of Jesus's ministry.

Matthew and Mark also tell us about the women who travel with Jesus, but not until the cross. As Mark writes,

> There were also women looking on from a distance, among whom were Mary Magdalene, and Mary the mother of James the younger and Joses, and Salome. When he was in Galilee, they followed him

and ministered to him, and there were also many other women who came up with him to Jerusalem. (Mark 15:40–41)

Matthew also names individual women among the group who witness Jesus's crucifixion and who had traveled with him since the early days in Galilee:

There were also many women there, looking on from a distance, who had followed Jesus from Galilee, ministering to him, among whom were Mary Magdalene and Mary the mother of James and Joseph and the mother of the sons of Zebedee. (Matt. 27:55–56)

Matthew and Mark both name Mary Magdalene and Mary the mother of James and Joseph.[4] But they choose different women as their third eyewitnesses. This is not a mistake. As Matthew tells us, many of Jesus's female disciples witness his death. But each Gospel author mentions the women whose testimony he's accessed in particular. Just as three eulogies at a funeral will highlight different memories, so the Gospel authors consult multiple people who knew Jesus firsthand in order to compile their narratives. The women Luke mentions in Luke 8:1–3 are among "those who from the beginning were eyewitnesses and ministers of the word" (Luke 1:2). The next time he names women, he's telling a story unique to his Gospel in which Jesus specifically affirms female discipleship.

4.   Joses and Joseph were variant forms of the same name.

SITTING AT JESUS'S FEET

Jesus and his disciples had entered a village, and a woman named Martha welcomed Jesus into her house (Luke 10:38). Martha was the fourth most common name among Jewish women of that time and place. She had a sister named (you guessed it) Mary.[5] The story Luke tells about these sisters is often used like a biblical personality test: "Are you a #1, The Activator, like Martha, or a #2, The Contemplator, like Mary?" But this interpretation misses the point. The story is not about two personality types. It's about two responses to Jesus, and Jesus's validation of female discipleship.

Having invited Jesus into her house, Martha was "distracted with much serving" (v. 40). The word Luke uses for Martha's "serving" comes from the same verb as the one he used to describe the women who "provided for" Jesus in Luke 8:3. But in this context, it is clearly referring to domestic duties. So, does this story support the interpretation that Jesus's female followers were just along to cook and clean? Not at all. While Martha was "distracted with serving," Mary "sat at the Lord's feet and listened to his teaching" (10:39).

Sitting at someone's feet is a posture of discipleship. The apostle Paul, for instance, describes himself as having been "educated at the feet of Gamaliel" (Acts 22:3). As New Testament scholar Darrell Bock puts it, "the

---

5. About six percent of Jewish women in the region were called Martha. See Bauckham, *Beloved Disciple*, 175.

picture of a woman in the disciple's position, at the feet of Jesus, would be startling in a culture where women did not receive formal teaching from a rabbi."[6] Maybe this Mary was emboldened to sit at Jesus's feet by seeing Mary Magdalene, Joanna, Susanna, and the other women among Jesus's disciples. As so often happens when Jesus lets controversial people in, he gets critiqued for letting Mary take that place. But in this story, the challenge doesn't come from the Pharisees, who are always eager to find fault with Jesus, or from Jesus's male disciples, who often misconstrue him. It comes from Martha.

Martha says to Jesus, "Lord, do you not care that my sister has left me to serve alone? Tell her then to help me" (Luke 10:40). In one sense, it's a reasonable request. Why should Martha be left with all the work while Mary sits around? Who does Mary think she is? But Jesus replies with a gentle rebuke not to Mary, as requested, but to Martha: "Martha, Martha, you are anxious and troubled about many things, but one thing is necessary. Mary has chosen the good portion, which will not be taken away from her" (vv. 41–42).

Jesus's doubling of Martha's name communicates tenderness. The only other time Jesus speaks like this to an individual in Luke is when he says, "Simon, Simon, behold, Satan demanded to have you, that he might sift you like wheat, but I have prayed for you that your faith may not fail" (Luke 22:31–32). Jesus's lament over Jerusalem

6. Darrell Bock, *Luke: 9:51–24:53*, vol. 2, Baker Exegetical Commentary on the New Testament (Grand Rapids, MI: Baker Academic, 1996), 1037.

captures a similar blend of love and sadness: "Jerusalem, Jerusalem, the city that kills the prophets and stones those who are sent to it! How often would I have gathered your children together as a hen gathers her brood under her wings, and you were not willing" (Luke 13:34).[7] Jesus's address to Martha is heartfelt. If he'd spoken it in English today, he might have said, "Oh, Martha!"

The rest of Jesus's response connects both with the words Martha has just uttered and also with words spoken centuries before. The immediate link is between literal and spiritual food. Martha is serving her guests a meal, while Mary has chosen the "good portion"—or "right meal"—by learning from Jesus.[8] But Jesus's words also reach back to the Hebrew hymnbook. In Psalm 16:5, King David declares, "The LORD is my chosen portion and my cup," while in Psalm 73, Asaph asks, "Whom have I in heaven but you? And there is nothing on earth that I desire besides you. My flesh and my heart may fail, but God is the strength of my heart and my portion forever" (Ps. 73:25–26). The Bible's longest psalm reiterates the point: "The LORD is my portion" (119:57). Martha thinks she's serving Jesus by giving him a meal. But Jesus clarifies that he's the one serving the real food—and Mary is right to sit at his table.

---

7. Darrel Bock includes the disciples saying, "Master, master" to Jesus before he calms the storm (Luke 8:24) as another example of a double address communicating strong emotion. See Bock, *Luke*, 1042.

8. Bock offers "the right meal" as a paraphrase of the good portion. See Bock, *Luke*, 1042.

How do we see Jesus through these sisters' eyes in Luke's Gospel? We see him as the one who welcomes women and defends their right to learn from him. We also see him as the one who gives us so much more than we could ever give to him.

WOMEN WHOM JESUS LOVED

People are often shocked by my lack of knowledge of celebrities. I once confused Beyoncé with Adele. Another time—even though I'd lived in New England for years—a friend had to explain to me that Tom Brady was not, in fact, a baseball player. How we introduce someone depends on whether we expect our audience to know who they are, and my friends have learned to assume nothing. But when John introduces Mary and Martha of Bethany, he does so in a way that assumes his readers have already heard of them:

> Now a certain man was ill, Lazarus of Bethany, the village of Mary and her sister Martha. It was Mary who anointed the Lord with ointment and wiped his feet with her hair, whose brother Lazarus was ill. (John 11:1–2)

In first-century Jewish culture, women were often identified by their relationship with a close male relative. But John reverses this and introduces us to Lazarus as Mary and Martha's brother. In fact, John seems to suggest that Mary (likely the younger of the sisters) was the most well known, and references something Mary did as if his readers would have heard of it before. That incident is recorded in Matthew, Mark, and in the next chapter of John. We'll explore it shortly. But here, at the beginning of John 11, we see these sisters sending an SOS to Jesus: "Lord, he whom you love is ill" (John 11:3).

This message is revealing. Mary and Martha do not call their brother "Lazarus," but "he whom you love." John refers to himself as "the disciple whom Jesus loved" (John 13:23; 19:26; 20:2; 21:7), but this verse highlights that he isn't unique in being loved by Jesus. And before we conclude that Jesus loves his male disciples most, John emphasizes Jesus's love for the sisters: "Now Jesus loved Martha and her sister and Lazarus" (John 11:5). The Greek word John uses here is *agapao*—the same word Jesus uses to describe the Father's love for him (John 10:17).[9] Jesus loves these siblings in the most profound way. This love makes Jesus's response to Mary and Martha's message jarring: "Now Jesus loved Martha and her sister and Lazarus. So, when we heard that Lazarus was ill, he stayed two days longer in the place where he was" (John 11:5–6). If we look through Mary's and Martha's eyes in this moment, we see Jesus as the one who has the power to heal their brother, but who chooses not to come when they cry out.

9. The author of John uses both these words at different times to describe Jesus's love for him. John 13:23; 21:7, 20 use *agapao* whereas John 20:2 uses *phileo*.

Days go by, and Jesus doesn't show. Perhaps the sisters think he hasn't come because it's dangerous. Bethany was only two miles away from Jerusalem, and when Jesus finally proposes to his disciples that they do go back down south, his disciples respond, "Rabbi, the Jews were just now seeking to stone you, and are you going there again?" (v. 8). But Jesus's decision not to come when he first got Mary and Martha's message had nothing to do with the risk to his life. Rather, he delayed so that God might be glorified (v. 4), and so that his disciples might believe (vv. 14–15).

When Jesus finally arrives at Bethany, Lazarus has already been in the tomb for four days. Martha hears that he has come and goes out to meet him. But Mary remains seated in the house. Martha says to Jesus, "Lord, if you had been here, my brother would not have died. But even now I know that whatever you ask from God, God will give you" (vv. 21–22). These words proclaim extraordinary faith. Lazarus is dead and buried. But even now she knows her Lord can heal him. We might expect at this point that Jesus would go with her straight to Lazarus's grave. Instead, he takes the time to teach this tearstained woman, whom he loves: "Your brother will rise again" (v. 23). Many first-century Jews believed that, on the final judgment day, God would raise them from the dead. So, Martha responds, "I know that he will rise again in the resurrection on the last day" (v. 24). But resurrection at the end of time is not what Martha is longing for. She'd sent for Jesus so that he could heal Lazarus. Now, she wants her Lord to bring him back to life. Jesus responds with some of the most astonishing words in all the Scriptures: "I am the resurrection and the life. Whoever believes in me, though he die, yet shall he live, and everyone who lives and believes in me shall never die. Do you believe this?" (vv. 25–26).

This is one of many moments in the Gospels where the idea that Jesus is *just* a good teacher gets smashed on the ground like a piece of cheap pottery. Good teachers do not claim to be the resurrection and the life, the source of life itself, the one without whom life is death, and with whom even death is life. But that's what Jesus claims. In this moment with Martha, Jesus claims that faith in him can conquer death itself. Martha's trust in Jesus is not just a means to an end, to bring her brother back. It is the source of her own life as well.

Faithful Jew that Martha is, she doubtless hears in Jesus's words an echo of the words God spoke to Moses many centuries before. God called Moses to go back to Egypt and to set God's people free. When Moses asked him for his name, the Lord replied, "I AM WHO I AM" and added, "Say this to the people of Israel: 'I AM has sent me to you'" (Ex. 3:14).[10] Jesus in John's Gospel evokes this holy name of God again and again. "I am the bread of life"

---

10. The divine name, transliterated *Yahweh*, is a form of the Hebrew verb "to be" used in the expression "I AM." For Jews, God's covenant name was so holy that it was never read aloud. Instead, they substituted *Adonai* which means "my Lord." The Greek translation of the Old Testament rendered *Yahweh* with the Greek word *kurios*—"Lord." Following this practice, most English translations of the Bible substitute "the LORD," using small capital letters.

(John 6:35, 41, 48, 51); "I am the light of the world" (8:12); "before Abraham was, I am" (8:58); "I am the door of the sheep" (10:7, 9); "I am the good shepherd" (10:11, 14); "I am the way, the truth, and the life" (14:6); "I am the true vine" (15:1, 5). Almost all of Jesus's "I am" statements are spoken to groups. "I am the resurrection and the life" is one of only two exceptions. As we'll see in chapter 3, the other "I am" statement spoken to an individual is also spoken to a woman. Martha had once resented Mary for sitting at Jesus's feet with the other disciples. Now, in an astounding act of grace, Jesus speaks some of his most world-transforming words to her alone.

Before he came to Bethany, Jesus told his disciples that he was glad for their sake that Lazarus had died, so that they might believe (John 11:14–15). But in this moment, he asks one female disciple for her response to his earthshaking claim: "Do you believe this?" Martha responds, "Yes, Lord; I believe that you are the Christ, the Son of God, who is coming into the world" (v. 27).

In moments of struggle, I've often muttered Jesus's claim and asked myself his question. A few years ago, in a period of intense relational turmoil—as I felt the psychological floor fall away under my feet—I stood in my bedroom clinging onto my dresser and rehearsed, "I am the resurrection and the life." "Do you believe this?" You see, if it's true, nothing that can happen in my life on earth can rob me of that everlasting life. And if it's false, nothing in my life on earth ultimately matters anyway. Either everything ends in death, or Jesus is the resurrection and the life.

How do we see Jesus through Martha's eyes in this moment? We see him as the one who can bring life back to her brother, as she craves. But also as the one who is himself the resurrection and the life. Just as God revealed himself to Moses as the one who simply *is*, so Jesus reveals himself to Martha as the one who in himself embodies life. To trust in Jesus is to live. It's not that Jesus *isn't* a good teacher. When Martha goes to get Mary, she says, "The Teacher is here and is calling for you" (v. 28). Jesus is a good teacher as surely as the sun is a source of light. But he's not *only* that. Just as our whole planet circles round the sun, so we should orient our lives around the Son of God, the Christ, who came into our world to summon us from death to life.

JESUS WEEPS

It would be easy to conclude from Jesus's words that we should cut our losses in this world and just stop caring. If Jesus is the resurrection and the life, let's step away from all the things that hurt and disassociate from suffering. If, as Buddhism teaches, the root of suffering is attachment, maybe we can pull the root and rid ourselves of the rotted tooth of pain. But John won't let us draw that inference. When Mary hears the teacher is calling for her, she gets up quickly and goes to him (John 11:29). Jesus still hasn't entered the village. Martha, in her eagerness, caught him on his way. When Mary arrives, she falls at his feet and repeats her sister's words: "Lord, if you had been here, my brother would not have died" (v. 32). How does Jesus respond to these words of lament? When Jesus sees Mary weeping, and the other Jews who had come with her also weeping, he is "deeply moved in his spirit and greatly troubled" (v. 33). He asks where Lazarus's body has been laid. And then he weeps (v. 35).

How do we see Jesus through Mary's reddened eyes in this moment? We see him as the one who could have saved her brother, but who let him die instead—and also as the one who weeps with her in her distress. Some of the bystanders saw the tears on Jesus's face and said, "See how he loved him" (v. 36). But others had a reasonable question: "Could not he who opened the eyes of the blind man also have kept this man from dying? (v. 37). The answer to their question is yes, and Mary knows it. But far from being callous to her pain, Jesus enters in.

If you have been a Christian for a while, my guess is you can think of times when you've cried to God for help and felt like you got nothing back. You've prayed for healing and it hasn't come. You've sent for Jesus and felt quite alone. But when, at long last, Jesus comes to Mary, he sheds tears with her. He hadn't stayed away because he didn't care. He stayed away because he *did* care. The best thing he could give these siblings, whom he profoundly loved, was not immediate answer to their prayers, but revelation of himself.

When Jesus comes to Lazarus's tomb, he's deeply moved again, and he tells them to take the stone away that covered up the entrance to the grave. Martha voices the unpalatable truth: "Lord, by this time there will be an odor, for he has been dead four days" (v. 39). Lazarus is dead and buried and rotting in his tomb. But Jesus says, "Did I not tell you that if you believed you would see the glory of God?" (v. 40). So, they roll the stone away. Jesus prays—for the benefit of those who are watching the action unfold—and then he cries out with a loud voice, "Lazarus, come out" (vv. 41–43). And so, John writes, "The man who had died came out, his hands and feet bound with linen strips, and his face wrapped with a cloth" (v. 44).

How do we see Jesus through Mary's and Martha's eyes as they watch their brother walk out of his tomb? We see him as the one who weeps with us in our distress, but also as the one who can call a dead man back to life. Jesus's power to raise Lazarus supports his staggering claim to Martha that he truly *is* the resurrection and the life. Many of the Jews who witness this believe in Jesus too (v. 45). But some go to the Pharisees and tell them what he's done (v. 46). This triggers a gathering of the chief priests and the Pharisees to plot Jesus's death. But rather than this being a disastrous turn of events, it's simply the next step in Jesus's plan: the one who is the resurrection and the life has come to die.

ANOINTED FOR BURIAL

As we saw earlier, when John introduces Mary and Martha, he writes, "It was Mary who anointed the Lord with ointment and wiped his feet with her hair" (John 11:2). It is clearly a well-known incident. But John's version of the story is notably different from Matthew's and Mark's. Mark tells the first part of the story like this:

> And while [Jesus] was at Bethany in the house of Simon the leper, as he was reclining at table, a woman came with an alabaster flask of ointment of pure nard, very costly, and she broke the flask and poured it over his head. (Mark 14:3)

Like Mark and Matthew, John locates the scene in Bethany. But where Mark and Matthew name the host as "Simon the leper," John doesn't mention the host at all:

> Six days before the Passover, Jesus therefore came to Bethany, where Lazarus was, whom Jesus had raised from the dead. So they gave a dinner for him there. Martha served, and Lazarus was one of those reclining with him at table. Mary therefore took a pound of expensive ointment made from pure nard, and anointed the feet of Jesus and wiped his feet with her hair. The house was filled with the fragrance of the perfume. (John 12:1–3)

Unlike Matthew and Mark, who leave her anonymous, John identifies the woman who did the anointing as Mary of Bethany. Rather than saying she poured ointment over his head, John says she anointed Jesus's feet. Examining the differences between these accounts will help us understand how the Gospel authors select and organize their material—like different film directors making their own distinctive cut.

First, the fact that Mary, Martha, and Lazarus are all present in John's version—and even that ever-industrious Martha is serving—need not mean that they are hosting the dinner (v. 2). If anything, Lazarus being among those reclining with Jesus suggests that he is *not* the owner of the house.[11] The host, whom Mark calls "Simon the leper," likely experienced Jesus's power to heal, as a current leper would not be able to host a dinner party. Presumably, multiple Bethany-based disciples got together to host their Lord. But what should we make of the fact that Mark and Matthew say the woman anointed Jesus's head, while John says she anointed his feet? Again, this need not be a contradiction. In Mark's version, Jesus says "she has anointed my body," implying that she didn't only anoint his head (Mark 14:8). But while Mark and Matthew focus our attention on the anointing of Jesus's head, which evokes the anointing of kings in the Old Testament, John highlights Mary's humble devotion in anointing Jesus's feet and wiping them with her hair.[12]

In all three Gospel accounts, the woman is criticized for her actions and Jesus strongly defends her. Mark writes,

---

11. See Craig L. Blomberg, *The Historical Reliability of John's Gospel* (Downers Grove, IL: IVP Academic, 2001), 176.
12. See Bauckham, *Beloved Disciple*, 188.

There were some who said to themselves indignantly, "Why was the ointment wasted like that? For this ointment could have been sold for more than three hundred denarii and given to the poor." And they scolded her. But Jesus said, "Leave her alone. Why do you trouble her? She has done a beautiful thing to me. For you always have the poor with you, and whenever you want, you can do good for them. But you will not always have me. She has done what she could; she has anointed my body beforehand for burial. And truly, I say to you, wherever the gospel is proclaimed in the whole world, what she has done will be told in memory of her." (Mark 14:4–9; see also Matt. 26:6–13)

The extravagance of Jesus's defense matches the extravagance of Mary's actions. He says she has done "a beautiful thing," and he prophesies that wherever the gospel is proclaimed in all the world, her story will be told in her memory. But instead of receiving the anointing of his head as recognition of his kingship, Jesus receives it as anointing for burial. Jesus is headed for death. He knows the path into his kingdom passes through the cross.

John's Gospel not only identifies the woman who anointed Jesus as Mary of Bethany, but also identifies her critic:

But Judas Iscariot, one of [Jesus's] disciples (he who was about to betray him), said, "Why was this ointment not sold for three hundred denarii and given to the poor?" He said this, not because he cared about the poor, but because he was a thief, and having charge of the moneybag he used to help himself to what was put into it. Jesus said, "Leave her alone, so that she may keep it for the day of my burial. For the poor you always have with you, but you do not always have me." (John 12:4–8)

Mary of Bethany's faithful devotion to Jesus is starkly contrasted with Judas's betrayal. While Mary spends her money lavishing love on Jesus, Judas steals from Jesus's ministry—money likely provided by disciples like Joanna—and then takes money from Jesus's enemies to betray him. Mary of Bethany is the disciple that Judas Iscariot should have been.

In Mark's account, despite neither Mary nor Judas being named, the contrast between Judas and the woman is still drawn. Mark frequently nestles one story between two parts of another to highlight a connection, and Mark's account of the woman who anointed Jesus is sandwiched between Judas's betrayal of Jesus—the chief priests and scribes "seeking how to arrest [Jesus] by stealth and kill him" (Mark 14:1)—and Judas's offer to hand over Jesus in exchange for money (vv. 10–11). As Jesus predicted, Mary of Bethany is remembered to this day for what she did. So is Judas. Indeed, while John gives a shorter summary of Jesus's response, pulling different strands from what he said, John's naming of Mary in this moment fulfills the prophecy that Mark recorded about her always being remembered for her actions.

How do we see Jesus through Mary of Bethany's eyes? We see him as the one who merits all of her extravagant love, the one on whom nothing can be wasted. We see him as the one who—once again—defends her from critique. We see him as the one who sees her beauty in her actions, and who validates her love with honor (Mark 14:6–9). Mary "sat at [Jesus's] feet" when he first came to Martha's house in Bethany (Luke 10:39). She "fell at his feet" and wept when he came to her after Lazarus's death (John 11:32). Now, she pours ointment on his feet and wipes them with her hair (John 12:3). Mary of Bethany knows her place: at Jesus's feet, where a disciple belongs.

Unlike Mary of Magdalene, Joanna, Susanna, and many other women, Mary and Martha of Bethany did not travel with Jesus. But they were nonetheless among his closest followers. In these sisters, we see two women Jesus loved. One received his everlasting commendation. The other received some of the most astonishing words he ever spoke. Did Jesus have female disciples? Yes, he absolutely did. And 2,000 years later, wherever the Gospels are read all over the world, their stories are told.

DISCUSSION QUESTIONS

Getting Started: Who is someone you enjoy "following," maybe by following them on social media, reading their books, watching or listening to their show, or consuming their art?

1. What does naming someone in the Gospels often indicate about them? How does this influence the way we understand the stories of the named women who followed Jesus?
2. What kind of women became Jesus's disciples?
3. What do we know about Mary Magdalene? Why is she an unlikely disciple?
4. How does the inclusion of Joanna in Luke's Gospel refute some common assumptions about how Jesus viewed his female disciples?
5. How do the women in this chapter shape your understanding of what it means to be a disciple or follower of Jesus?
6. When have you struggled with God not answering your prayers the way you hoped? How can Jesus's interactions with Mary and Martha surrounding Lazarus's death affect the way you respond to that heartbreak?
7. How have you been tempted to withhold something from Jesus? How does the story of Mary pouring expensive ointment on Jesus free you to worship lavishly?
8. How do you see Jesus most meaningfully through the eyes of these women?

Going Deeper: Read John 11:1–44.

1. How many times does a form of the word "die" or "death" appear in this passage?

2. What does Jesus say about Lazarus's illness in verse 4? How does Jesus's statement in verse 14 seem contradictory? How do verses 25 and 44 bring resolution to this tension?

3. Why did Jesus let Lazarus die based on verses 4–6, 15, 25–27, and 40–42? What do these events reveal about the nature of being a disciple of Jesus Christ?

CHAPTER 3

NOURISHMENT

"I HATE FOOD."

My 3-year-old, Luke, was going through a phase. "I hate food" at lunchtime. "I hate drink" when offered his cup. Even, in a conspiratorial whisper, "I hate people." But on hearing I'd made pasta for his dinner, "I love you! I'll be happy as a pig!"

We may not voice our feelings quite as forcefully as Luke does. But my guess is that, for most of us, our relationship with food and drink is mixed. Good food can bring us joy, especially when shared with those we love. But there's a shadow side. We're plagued with body-image stress in a world of idealized thinness for women and fat-free muscularity for men. We look to food or drink for comfort or to cover up our pain—to give us the illusion of control or a means of escape.

The first-century Near Eastern world in which the Gospels are set was very different from the 21st-century Western world in which I live. For most women then, the most pressing question when it came to food and drink was not, "How much is too much?" but, "Is there enough?" This is still the question for many women around the world today. But whether we struggle with want or excess, our basic human need for nourishment connects us with all people throughout time. In this chapter, we'll examine four conversations Jesus has with women that hinge on food and drink. As Jesus engages with these women about spiritual water, bread, and wine, we see him through their eyes as the one from whom all real nourishment comes. We also see him as the only one who really knows us at our best and worst, and who gives us an identity apart from anything that social media could capture or old age could steal.

WATER INTO WINE

My husband and I got married twice. First, in June in Cambridge, U.K., and then in October, in Oklahoma City. In England, weddings come with alcohol. Traditionally the bride's family pays for the wedding and the groom's family pays for the wine. But in Oklahoma, where Bryan grew up, there's a strong tradition among Christians of not drinking alcohol at all, so our Oklahoma wedding was a dry event. I get both views. The Bible clearly warns us against drunkenness, and whole lives and families can be derailed by alcohol.[1] For many,

---

1. For example, in his letter to the church in Ephesus, the apostle Paul writes, "Do not get drunk with wine, for that is debauchery, but be filled

abstinence is wise. But the first miracle recorded in John's Gospel is not a healing or a resurrection. It's the story of when Jesus turned gallons of water at a wedding into the most delicious wine.

This story is the first time that Jesus's mother Mary is mentioned in John. Jesus and Mary are both at a wedding in Cana, a small town north of Nazareth, and the wine has run out. Mary finds her son and says, "They have no wine" (John 2:3). Jesus's response sounds strange to us: "Woman," he replies, "what does this have to do with me? My hour has not yet come" (v. 4). Jesus addressing his mother as "woman" strikes us as disrespectful. But it's not. The resonances are not equivalent, but just as calling someone "man" or "girl" in American English is friendly and informal, so calling someone "woman" in first-century Jewish culture was not derogatory. A more literal translation of what he says next would be, "what is that to me and you?" Neither Jesus nor his mother is hosting the wedding, so the wine running out is not their problem. But Jesus adds an odd remark: "My hour has not yet come." In John's Gospel, Jesus's "hour" points to his crucifixion.[2] Perhaps Jesus means that revealing his

---

with the Spirit" (Eph. 5:18).

2. In John 7:30 and 8:20, Jesus escaped arrest "because his hour had not yet come," while in John 12:23, anticipating the crucifixion, Jesus declares that "the hour has come for the Son of Man to be glorified," and adds, "Now is my soul troubled. And what shall I say? 'Father, save me from this hour'? But for this purpose I have come to this hour" (12:27). See also "Jesus knew that his hour had come to depart out of this world to the Father" (13:1) and "Father, the hour has come; glorify your Son so that the Son may glorify you" (17:1).

power now will cause the kind of trouble that could get him killed, and it isn't time for that yet. But instead of replying to Jesus, Mary just says to the servants, "Do whatever he tells you" (v. 5). She doesn't know what Jesus will do, but she knows that the right response is total trust in Jesus's direction.

Jesus tells the servants to fill six 20- to 30-gallon jars with water. Once they're filled to the brim, Jesus says, "Now draw some out and take it to the master of the feast" (v. 8). When the master of the feast tastes the liquid, he calls the bridegroom and says, "Everyone serves the good wine first, and when people have drunk freely, then the poor wine. But you have kept the good wine until now" (v. 10). The bridegroom would've been responsible for providing the wine for the wedding. But Jesus steps into the bridegroom's role and provides not only *more* wine, but *better* wine than the guests had in the first place. This hint of Jesus's identity is developed more fully in the next chapter of John, when John the Baptist says of Jesus,

> The one who has the bride is the bridegroom. The friend of the bridegroom, who stands and hears him, rejoices greatly at the bridegroom's voice. Therefore this joy of mine is now complete. (John 3:29)[3]

---

3. See also in Mark, when the Pharisees ask Jesus why his disciples did not fast: "Can the wedding guests fast while the bridegroom is with them?" (Mark 2:19).

The Old Testament portrays God as a loving, faithful husband to Israel, his all-too-often-faithless wife.[4] In the New Testament, Jesus steps in as the Bridegroom.

Jesus's water-to-wine miracle points both to his identity as the Bridegroom and also to God's joyful provision for his people. The Bible promises a future feast of rich food and fine wine. For example, Isaiah declares,

> On this mountain the LORD of hosts will make for all peoples
>> a feast of rich food, a feast of well-aged wine,
>> of rich food full of marrow, of aged wine well refined. (Isa. 25:6)[5]

As with so many other things God made, food and drink at their most sumptuous point to his lavish love for us. When Jesus provides the finest wine for the wedding in Cana, he shows he is the source of that future feast: the feast where all our thirst will be quenched and our desire for laughter, connection, and joy will be fulfilled.

His mother, Mary, knows what he can do, so she calls on him. But Jesus's next conversation with a woman in John's Gospel is with a total stranger.

---

4. See, for example, Isa. 54:5; Jer. 2:2; 3:1; Hos. 2; Ezek. 16.
5. See also the Lord's invitation later in Isaiah: "Come, everyone who thirsts, come to the waters; and he who has no money, come, buy and eat! Come, buy wine and milk without money and without price" (Isa. 55:1).

LIVING WATER

We might expect a conversation with his mother to be Jesus's longest dialogue with a woman. After all, she would be the most appropriate woman for an unmarried rabbi to talk to—especially in private. But instead, Jesus's longest recorded private conversation with anyone in the Gospels is with a woman Jewish men would have avoided at all costs. This woman is the first person in John's Gospel to whom Jesus explicitly reveals himself as the Christ, and she is the last person with whom a respectable rabbi should have been spending time alone.

Jesus and his disciples are on the way back from Judea (in the south) to Galilee (in the north) when they stop near a Samaritan town. Samaria lay smack in between Judea and Galilee, but Jews would often take a circuitous route to avoid it because of the hostility between Jews and Samaritans. After the Assyrians conquered the northern kingdom of Israel in 722 BC, most of the resident Israelites were deported. Some were left and intermarried with foreigners relocated there from other parts of the Assyrian Empire (2 Kings 17:24–41). This intermarrying produced the Samaritans. Jews saw Samaritans as both racially and religiously contaminated. Like the Jews, they worshiped the Lord, but they only recognized the Bible's first five books, and while Jews worshiped at the Jerusalem temple on Mount Zion, the Samaritans built an alternative temple on Mount Gerizim. The Jews destroyed this Samaritan temple in 128 BC, cementing the enmity between the two groups. But instead of steering his disciples clear of Samaritan turf, Jesus leads them right into it.

It's midday and, tired from the journey, Jesus sits down at Jacob's well to rest. Water drawing was traditionally women's work, and to avoid the blistering heat, the women came in the early morning or late afternoon. But as Jesus sits by the well at noon, one Samaritan woman comes to draw, and Jesus asks her for a drink (John 4:7). John raises the tension by telling us that the disciples have gone into town to buy food (v. 8). Jesus is apparently alone. He's crossing segregation lines by even talking to this woman, let alone asking her to share her drinking vessel. "How is it," she replies, "that you, a Jew, ask for a drink from me, a woman of Samaria?" (v. 9). In case his readers aren't familiar with quite how taboo this would be, John adds, "For Jews have no dealings with Samaritans" (v. 9). As we look through this Samaritan woman's eyes in this moment, we see Jesus as a Jewish man trampling on the ethnic and social barriers of his day. Perhaps she wonders what he's *really* after. But Jesus isn't there for what he can take. He's there for what he can give.

"If you knew the gift of God," Jesus replies, "and who it is that is saying to you, 'Give me a drink,' you would have asked him, and he would have given you living water" (v. 10). The woman thinks the shocking thing about Jesus asking her for a drink is that he's crossing great social divides. But Jesus says what's *actually* shocking is that he's asking her for a drink, not vice versa. "Living water" could just mean fresh spring water. But the language also carried spiritual freight. Through the prophet

Jeremiah, God had lamented, "My people have committed two evils: they have forsaken me, the fountain of living waters, and hewed out cisterns for themselves, broken cisterns that can hold no water" (Jer. 2:13). Later, Jeremiah declares, "They have forsaken the LORD, the fountain of living water" (17:13). Sitting by a literal well, Jesus makes a theological point: he is the Lord, the source of living water.

The Samaritan woman doesn't get what Jesus means. But she still realizes that he's making a bold claim:

> Sir, you have nothing to draw water with, and the well is deep. Where do you get that living water? Are you greater than our father Jacob? He gave us the well and drank from it himself, as did his sons and his livestock. (John 4:11–12)

Both Jews and Samaritans considered themselves to be the true carriers of the flame passed down by Abraham through Isaac and Jacob, the father of the 12 tribes of Israel. Claiming to be greater than Jacob would be quite the boast. From this woman's perspective, the answer to her question has to be no. Surely this Jewish rabbi doesn't think he's greater than Jacob! But instead of answering her question, Jesus raises the stakes:

> Everyone who drinks of this water will be thirsty again, but whoever drinks of the water that I will give him will never be thirsty again. The water that I will

give him will become in him a spring of water welling up to eternal life. (vv. 13–14)

Jesus here presses more deeply into the metaphor from Jeremiah: he is the source of living water, and anyone who receives him will in turn become the location of a spring. Jesus will make the same point later in John's Gospel. Standing in the temple, he will cry, "If anyone thirsts, let him come to me and drink. Whoever believes in me, as the Scripture has said, 'Out of his heart will flow rivers of living water'" (John 7:37–38). But before declaring this in public to his fellow Jews in the most expected place, Jesus declares it in private to this foreign woman in the least expected place.

The Samaritan woman responds with a tangle of misunderstanding and hope: "Sir, give me this water, so that I will not be thirsty or have to come here to draw water" (John 4:15). She wants what Jesus says he has. But she can't see what he is really offering. So often, I find myself in this place: seeing Jesus as a means to an end, pleading with him for things I want—or even need. Perhaps you can relate. Maybe Jesus functions in your life like an ethereal Santa: someone to whom you can submit your wishlist, and who brings a tinge of magic to the fringes of your day-to-day life. But while Jesus is the source of every good thing we have, and loves to hear our prayers, if we knew the gift of God, and who we were talking to, we'd ask him, first and foremost, to give us himself.

Jesus's next move would strike her ancient and our modern ears quite differently. "Go, call your husband,"

he says, "and come here" (v. 16). From a first-century perspective, this request is overdue. This solo conversation
would be flat-out inappropriate. Much better to have her
husband there. From our perspective, it may sound misogynistic—as if Jesus doesn't want to talk to her in her
own right. But as the conversation unfolds, we find that
both these interpretations of Jesus's words are wrong.
The woman replies, "I have no husband" (v. 17) and Jesus
shows his own cards by revealing hers:

> You are right in saying, "I have no husband"; for you
> have had five husbands, and the one you now have
> is not your husband. What you have said is true.
> (vv. 17–18)

Why does Jesus say this? Is his goal to shame her? No.
He's telling her he knew her history when he first asked
her for a drink. This woman might have been morally disgraced: passed around from man to man—at this
point, in her culture, not much better than a prostitute.
Or she may have been widowed multiple times and now
be living in a *de facto* marriage. We don't know all the
details. But Jesus does. And he doesn't walk away from
this sexually suspicious foreigner. Instead, he uses what
he knows of her identity to reveal more of his.

How do we see Jesus through this woman's eyes? She
tells us: "Sir, I perceive that you are a prophet" (v. 19). The
Samaritan woman sees that Jesus is a prophet because he
sees all of her history. This foreigner is not beneath the

notice of the Son of God. Jesus knows her life story, just as he knows yours and mine.

Realizing that she's talking with a prophet, the Samaritan woman raises a theological question: "Our fathers worshiped on this mountain, but you say that in Jerusalem is the place where people ought to worship" (v. 20). The mountain she's referring to, Mount Gerizim, would have been visible from Jacob's well. But rather than arguing for Jerusalem as the right place for worship, Jesus replies,

> Woman, believe me, the hour is coming when neither on this mountain nor in Jerusalem will you worship the Father. You worship what you do not know; we worship what we know, for salvation is from the Jews. But the hour is coming, and is now here, when the true worshipers will worship the Father in spirit and truth, for the Father is seeking such people to worship him. God is spirit, and those who worship him must worship in spirit and truth. (vv. 21–24)

At the wedding in Cana, Jesus told his mother that his hour had not yet come (John 2:4). Now, he tells this Samaritan woman that "the hour is coming" when God's true worshipers will worship not in temples, but in spirit and in truth. In fact, he says, the hour is here. "I know that Messiah is coming (he who is called Christ)," she replies. "When he comes, he will tell us all things" (John 4:25). Translated literally, Jesus replies, "I am, the (one) speaking to you" (v. 26).

This word-for-word translation comes out awkwardly in English, so it's often broken up in our Bibles. But as New Testament scholar Craig Evans observes, Jesus's statement is "emphatic and unusual" in the original Greek as well.[6] Smoothing it out in translation masks the fact that this is the first of Jesus's "I am" statements. As we saw in the last chapter, almost all the other "I am" statements in John are spoken to groups. The two exceptions are Jesus's words to Martha—"I am the resurrection and the life" (John 11:25)—and his response to this Samaritan woman. This is the first time in John that Jesus explicitly declares he's the Messiah. And as he does so, Jesus makes an even more extraordinary claim.

Each of Jesus's "I am" statements give us fresh insight into who he is. At first, his words to the Samaritan woman seem like an exception. But if we look more closely, Jesus *is* giving us more insight about his identity when he says to the Samaritan woman, "I am, the (one) speaking to you." Jesus claims he's the Messiah and the one true covenant God. But he is also the one who is speaking to this sexually suspect, foreign woman. He could have just said "I am he!" But as we look at Jesus through this woman's eyes, we see him as the long-promised King and everlasting God, who chooses to converse with her. However insignificant we think we are, however much of an outsider we might feel, however many times we've

6.   See Craig A. Evans, *The Bible Knowledge Background Commentary: John's Gospel, Hebrews–Revelation* (Colorado Springs: David C. Cook, 2005).

been abandoned and cast out, here we see Jesus as the God who wants to spend his time with us.

Right when Jesus reveals to the woman who he is, his disciples come back. They're amazed that he's talking to her, but they don't dare to ask him why (John 4:27). Then John gives us this beautifully evocative detail: "So the woman left her water jar and went away into town and said to the people, 'Come, see a man who told me all I ever did. Can this be the Christ?'" (vv. 28–29). When Jesus called Simon Peter and Andrew, they left their nets and followed him (Matt. 4:18–20). When Jesus called James and John, they left their boat and their father and followed him (vv. 21–22). This woman leaves behind her water jar to go and tell the people of the town who Jesus is. What is her evidence for Jesus's identity as God's long-promised King? That he knew everything she ever did.

We all long to be deeply known and loved. But so often we feel the need to manage how much we're known, because if people really knew the truth about us—our darkest thoughts, our envy, our deceit, our lust, our failed relationships—we fear that we would not be loved. In Jesus, this woman met a man who knew her to the core. He could have ignored her at the well or pulled away. Instead, he met her deepest need and told her who he is.

Jesus's knowledge of this woman became central to her message about him. John tells us,

> Many Samaritans from that town believed in [Jesus] because of the woman's testimony, "He told me all

that I ever did." So when the Samaritans came to him, they asked him to stay with them, and he stayed there two days. And many more believed because of his word. They said to the woman, "It is no longer because of what you said that we believe, for we have heard for ourselves, and we know that this is indeed the Savior of the world." (John 4:39–42)

Through this woman's message about Jesus, people who were raised to hate the Jews came to hear this Jewish rabbi and asked him to stay with them. When he spoke to them as he had spoken to the woman at the well, they knew him as he truly is: the Savior of the world, the one whose living water is available to anyone who thirsts and comes to him.

CHILDREN'S BREAD

In Mark and Matthew, another conversation with a foreign woman emphasizes the universal scope of Jesus's mission. The scene is set in a Gentile region north of Galilee. Its immediate context is a confrontation Jesus has with Pharisees who complained that Jesus's disciples did not ritually wash their hands before eating. Jesus calls them hypocrites and explains that it's not what goes into your stomach that makes you unclean, but what comes out of your heart (Matt. 15:7–20; Mark 7:6–23). Then Jesus gets up and leaves for the Gentile region of Tyre and Sidon (Matt. 15:21; Mark 7:24).

When Jesus arrives, he wants to stay hidden for a time. But Mark tells us that "immediately a woman whose little daughter had an unclean spirit heard of him and came down and fell at his feet" (Mark 7:25). Mark emphasizes this woman's nationality: "the woman was a Gentile, a Syrophoenician by birth" (v. 26). Tyre and Sidon were in Phoenicia, so this is a way of communicating that she is a local in that region, and distinctly non-Jewish. Matthew makes the same point with another word by calling her "a Canaanite woman from that region" (Matt. 15:22). The Canaanites were the original inhabitants of the land God promised to the Israelites. They no longer existed as a distinct people group, but by calling this woman a Canaanite, Matthew emphasizes her ethnic and religious foreignness. This woman is an outsider through and through. And yet we find she has a better grasp on who Jesus is than the Jewish leaders Jesus just encountered.

In Matthew's account, the woman came to Jesus and cried out, "Have mercy on me, O Lord, Son of David; my daughter is severely oppressed by a demon" (v. 22). But just as when Mary and Martha first called him for help, Jesus didn't answer. This foreigner is not deterred. She keeps on asking, so much so that Jesus's disciples beg him, saying, "Send her away, for she is crying out after us" (vv. 22–23). But instead of responding to their request, Jesus finally replies to the woman herself: "I was sent only to the lost sheep of the house of Israel" (v. 24). Jesus uses this language earlier in Matthew, when he sends his 12 apostles out to preach and heal with the instruction, "Go nowhere among the Gentiles and enter no town of the Samaritans, but go rather to the lost sheep of the house of Israel" (Matt. 10:5–6). The Jews were to receive the message of salvation first. But the woman will not be put off. She comes and kneels before Jesus, saying simply, "Lord, help me" (Matt. 15:25). When my 3-year-old, Luke, isn't getting my attention, he sometimes comes and grabs my face and asks me something nose-to-nose. This woman is kneeling down before Jesus, but the effect is the same.

Jesus's reply sounds shocking to us: "It is not right to take the children's bread and throw it to the dogs" (v. 26). In the Old Testament, the Israelites were often called God's children. Conversely, Jews of Jesus's day would sometimes refer to Gentiles as dogs. Jesus's Jewish disciples might well have nodded along as Jesus spoke. But rather than recoiling at the insult, the woman picks up Jesus's metaphor, "Yes, Lord, yet even the dogs eat the crumbs that fall from their masters' table" (v. 27). Jesus has just come from the Pharisees, who were trying to teach Jesus a lesson about how his disciples should eat. He's called them "hypocrites" and "blind guides" (vv. 7, 14) who have no idea what they're talking about. But this woman understands what the Pharisees could not. She knows she has no right to sit at Jesus's table, and it's precisely those who know they have no right that Jesus welcomes in. He replies, "O woman, great is your faith! Be it done for you as you desire." And her daughter is healed instantly (v. 28).

Some commentators suggest that this Gentile woman changed Jesus's mind. But Jesus's inclusion of Gentiles has already been established earlier in Matthew by his interaction with a Roman centurion. He wanted Jesus to heal his servant, who was suffering terribly, but he knew he was not worthy to have Jesus come into his house. The man's humility and trust impressed Jesus so much that he said to his disciples,

> Truly, I tell you, with no one in Israel have I found such faith. I tell you, many will come from east and west and recline at table with Abraham, Isaac, and Jacob in the kingdom of heaven, while the sons of the kingdom will be thrown into the outer darkness. In that place there will be weeping and gnashing of teeth. (Matt. 8:10–12)

Jesus recognizes that his fellow Jews are the rightful heirs of the kingdom of God: the "sons of the kingdom" or, as he put it to the Syrophoenician woman, "the children." But any Jews who turn away from Jesus will be thrown out of the kingdom, while any Gentiles who accept him will be welcomed in. The Syrophoenician woman does not change Jesus's mind. Rather, their interaction gives her the opportunity to show her humble faith.

How do we see Jesus through this desperate Gentile woman's eyes? We see him as the Son of David, with the power to heal and save from spiritual disease, and as the one we don't deserve, but who will nonetheless show us mercy. We see that even the crumbs that fall from Jesus's table are enough for us, but that Jesus will welcome all who trust in him to the everlasting feast. The

Syrophoenician woman kneels before Jesus and makes a request for her child. The next woman to do this in Matthew is not only Jewish, she's the mother of two of Jesus's closest disciples. She might reasonably expect to have Jesus's ear. But as the scene unfolds, we see a very different outcome.

BITTER CUP

When Jesus calls James and John to follow him, they are in a boat with their father Zebedee, mending their nets. But on Jesus's summons, they immediately "left the boat and their father and followed [Jesus]" (Matt. 4:22). The brothers are referred to in all four Gospels as "the sons of Zebedee." No mention is made of their mother at this point. But after Jesus predicts his crucifixion and resurrection for the third time, Matthew writes, "Then the mother of the sons of Zebedee came up to him with her sons, and kneeling before him she asked him for something" (Matt. 20:20). Her first recorded words show that, like Jesus's apostles, she hasn't understood what Jesus's kingdom is about. Jesus asks her, "What do you want?" and she replies, "Say that these two sons of mine are to sit, one at your right hand and one at your left, in your kingdom" (v. 21). When Mark tells the story, he focuses our attention on James and John (Mark 10:35–40). Clearly, both mother and sons are united in their request. But Matthew foregrounds the mother's role.

How do we see Jesus through the eyes of the mother of the sons of Zebedee? We see her faith that Jesus is God's promised King and is the one who can grant privilege and prestige to his most faithful followers. If you're like me, perhaps you've sometimes looked at Jesus like this. You've knelt down before him not to worship, but to ask him to fulfill your desire for success. Perhaps this woman reasoned that she wasn't being selfish. After all, she wasn't wanting something for *herself*, just for her boys. But every parent knows how easy it can be to live our own dreams through our kids and tell ourselves that it's not selfishness.

Jesus answers this mother's request, "You do not know what you are asking. Are you able to drink the cup that I am to drink?" (Matt. 20:22). Jesus speaks in the plural, likely addressing all three, but it's James and John who answer his question: "We are able" (v. 22). They don't understand any more than their mother does. This woman thinks she is securing prestige for her sons. But Jesus says she's asking him for suffering.

The next time the sons of Zebedee are mentioned in Matthew is the night when Jesus is betrayed. He goes with his disciples to a place called Gethsemane and says to them, "Sit here, while I go over there and pray" (Matt. 26:36). But then he takes "Peter and the two sons of Zebedee" with him further on (v. 37). He says to them, "My soul is very sorrowful, even to death; remain here, and watch with me." And going a little farther he falls on his face and prays, "My Father, if it be possible, let this cup pass from me; nevertheless, not as I will, but as you will" (vv. 38–39).

In the Old Testament, the cup of Yahweh signified his judgment against sin. The prophet Jeremiah writes, "Thus the LORD, the God of Israel, said to me: 'Take from my hand this cup of the wine of wrath, and make all the nations to whom I send you drink it'" (Jer. 25:15). Shockingly, the first "nation" to whom the cup is passed is God's own people (v. 18). Isaiah, Habakkuk, and Ezekiel use the same metaphor (Isa. 51:17–22; Hab. 2:16; Ezek. 23:31). As Jesus faces the cross, he dreads this cup. Could James and John drink it? Not at all. In fact, while Jesus is pleading with his Father, James and John and all his other followers are fast asleep. But earlier that night, they *had* drunk wine from another cup. At dinner, Jesus took a cup, and when he had given thanks he gave it to his disciples, saying, "Drink of it, all of you, for this is my blood of the covenant, which is poured out for many for the forgiveness of sins" (Matt. 26:27–28). Because Jesus would drink the cup of God's wrath against sin, he was able to share the cup of his blood poured out for the forgiveness of sins. James and John would also go on to drink the cup of suffering as followers of Jesus. Indeed, we see James martyred in the book of Acts (Acts 12:2). The brothers reply to Jesus's question, "We are able." He says to them, "You will drink my cup, but to sit at my right hand and at my left is not mine to grant, but it is for those for whom it has been prepared by my Father" (Matt. 20:22–23).

The rest of Jesus's 12 apostles are angry when they hear of James and John's request. How dare they try to secure the top spots in Jesus's kingdom? But Jesus calls them all to himself and explains that greatness in his kingdom comes not with self-serving power, but with service. "Whoever would be great among you must be your servant," he declares, "and whoever would be first among you must be your slave, even as the Son of Man came not to be served but to serve, and to give his life as a ransom for many" (vv. 26–28). The mother of the sons of Zebedee must feel the force of this rebuke. She's got it absolutely wrong. But this is not the last we hear of her.

The mother of the sons of Zebedee is one of Matthew's named eyewitnesses of Jesus's crucifixion. We discover in that moment that she had followed him since the early days of his ministry in Galilee (Matt. 27:55–56). This woman saw the charge above his head, "This is Jesus, the King of the Jews" (v. 37). She saw the two robbers crucified with him, one on the right and one on the left (v. 38). She must have realized in that moment just how wrong she'd been. But she stuck with Jesus to the end, and likely later saw her two sons, James and John, become bold witnesses to Jesus as the risen Christ: the King who drank the cup and came into his kingdom through the cross.

'I THIRST'

The mother of the sons of Zebedee was not the only mother watching Jesus die. John's Gospel tells us Mary, Jesus's mother, was a witness of the crucifixion too. Mary had soothed the infant Jesus's cries with her milk. She'd seen the adult Jesus turning water into wine. Now, she sees the dying Jesus crying out in thirst:

After this, Jesus, knowing that all was now finished, said (to fulfill the Scripture), "I thirst." A jar full of sour wine stood there, so they put a sponge full of sour wine on a hyssop branch and held it to his mouth. When Jesus had received the sour wine, he said, "It is finished," and he bowed his head and gave up his spirit. (John 19:28–30)

How do we see Jesus through his mother's eyes in this moment? We see the one who had the power to turn 180 gallons of water from six stone jars into the finest wine experiencing thirst and receiving a mouthful of sour wine. We see the sword that pierced his mother's heart— as Simeon had prophesied—and the extraordinary price that Jesus paid so sinful folk like you and me could eat and drink and live with him forever.

We look to food and drink for life and comfort, for release and strength. Time and again in the Gospels, Jesus presents himself as food and drink. His first "I am" is spoken to the Samaritan woman at the well, after offering her living water. He makes his second "I am" statement after feeding 5,000 people with five loaves and two fish: "I am the bread of life," he said, "whoever comes to me shall not hunger, and whoever believes in me shall never thirst" (John 6:35). Jesus is the living water and the living bread. The nourishment he gives springs from his death. "Truly, truly, I say to you," Jesus explains, "unless you eat the flesh of the Son of Man and drink his blood, you have no life in you. Whoever feeds on my flesh and drinks my blood has eternal life, and I will raise him up on the last day" (vv. 53–54). I don't know how you feel about food and drink today. I don't know whether you hate food and drink for the struggle they present, or whether eating and drinking brings you joy. But I do know this: without Jesus, we will all starve. With him, we'll enjoy an everlasting, love-instilling, hope-fulfilling feast.

DISCUSSION QUESTIONS

Getting Started: What is your favorite beverage to enjoy on a hot day?

1. How does Jesus reveal his identity as the Bridegroom? Why is this title significant?
2. What are some of the factors that make Jesus's conversation with the woman at the well so controversial?
3. What does Jesus reveal about himself to the woman at the well?
4. What do the woman at the well and the woman who asked Jesus to heal her daughter have in common? What do Jesus's interactions with them reveal about the gospel?
5. Why do you think Jesus chose to use metaphors about food and drink to describe himself and what he offers? What do these metaphors reveal about his character?
6. Where in your life are you experiencing unsatisfied hunger?

7. How should seeing Jesus as the one from whom all real nourishment comes influence the way you relate to him now?

8. How do you see Jesus most meaningfully through the eyes of these women?

Going Deeper: Read John 4:1–42.

1. What are the two primary things Jesus reveals to the woman at the well in their conversation? See John 4:10.

2. What does Isaiah 44:3 equate with water poured out on thirsty land? How does this verse influence the way you understand the gift of God Jesus references in John 4:10? How might a Jewish audience respond to the fact that Jesus offers this gift to a Samaritan woman?

3. What role did the woman at the well play in the newfound belief of the other Samaritans? How does her role inform how we understand evangelism?

CHAPTER 4

HEALING

YESTERDAY IN CHURCH, I sat next to a friend of mine named Grace who likely has months left to live. She first had cancer 23 years ago, when her daughter was young. Now, it has come back to finish the job. Grace is Malaysian Chinese. Her husband, Raja, who died a decade ago, was Malaysian of South Indian heritage. He'd been diagnosed with a heart condition and recommended to have an operation with a 97 percent survival rate. It turned out he was in the 3 percent. Grace and Raja met in Sunday school as kids. When Grace first had cancer, she prayed for healing. This time, she hasn't. She's prayed for courage and for help, but not for healing. Despite being too young to die by Western standards, she feels "ready to be with the Lord." Singing to Jesus with a dying friend, who trusts him as her resurrection and her life, is sobering. The words taste different in your mouth when you're singing next to someone who will soon find out for sure if they are true.

I don't know how your medical report would read to-day. Perhaps you're in the prime of life and healthy to the core. Perhaps you're on the verge of death: "the undiscovered country from whose bourn," as Hamlet agonized, "no traveler returns."[1] Most likely, you're somewhere in between, with periodic aches and pains and bouts of sickness that drop in like uninvited guests. But all of us will die one day. What does Jesus have to do with us as we skip, hop, or crawl toward our end?

As we saw in chapter 1, when Luke first introduces us to Jesus's female disciples, he writes, "The twelve were with him, and also some women who had been healed of evil spirits and infirmities" (Luke 8:1–2). Curiously, the healing stories of the women Luke then names among Jesus's disciples are not told in the Gospels. We don't know what Joanna or Susanna had suffered from before they met with Jesus, or how Mary Magdalene had come to be healed from demonic possession. But we do know the stories of other women healed in the Gospels, and in this chapter, we will look at Jesus through their eyes.

PETER'S MOTHER-IN-LAW

Most people Jesus meets in the Gospels are unnamed, so it's no surprise that many of the women Jesus healed are unnamed too. In fact, among the healing stories

1. From Act III scene I of William Shakespeare's Hamlet, Prince of Denmark. See Herschel Baker, et al., eds., *The Riverside Shakespeare* (Boston & New York: Houghton Mifflin Company, 1997), 1208.

told of men in the Gospels, the only ones with names are the blind man Bartimaeus, who is only named by Mark (Mark 10:46); the high priest's servant Malchus, who is only named in John (John 18:10); and Lazarus. In all the stories told of Jesus healing women, the women are anonymous as well, except for one. And she's identified not by her name but by her relationship to one of Jesus's disciples.

The healing of Simon Peter's mother-in-law is the first story of physical healing in Mark's Gospel, and it comes hot on the heels of the first story of spiritual healing. Jesus was teaching in the synagogue in Capernaum when a man possessed by an unclean spirit cried out, "What have you to do with us, Jesus of Nazareth? Have you come to destroy us? I know who you are—the Holy One of God" (Mark 1:24). Jesus commands the spirit, "Be silent, and come out of him!" and the unclean spirit convulsed the man. Crying out in a loud voice, the spirit came out (vv. 25–26). This incident caused Jesus's fame to spread throughout the region of Galilee. Then Mark writes:

> And immediately [Jesus] left the synagogue and entered the house of Simon and Andrew, with James and John. Now Simon's mother-in-law lay ill with a fever, and immediately they told him about her. And he came and took her by the hand and lifted her up, and the fever left her, and she began to serve them. (vv. 29–31)

Most people Jesus heals in the Gospels are strangers. In this story, Jesus heals someone who was likely well known to him. The details are sparse. But the woman's reaction is significant: as soon as Jesus heals her, she serves.

Matthew, Mark, and Luke all tell the story, but we might wonder why. Of all the hundreds or thousands of people Jesus healed, why highlight this one? Did they simply want to reinforce a woman's role of serving? I don't think so. If we read this story within the web of the Gospels as a whole, we'll find it doesn't simply reinforce a woman's place. The verb for serving (*diakoneo*) that's applied to Peter's mother-in-law also describes the angels who ministered to Jesus after he was tempted in the wilderness (Mark 1:13; Matt. 4:11). It describes Jesus's female disciples (Luke 8:1–3). It describes Martha of Bethany when she serves while her sister Mary sits at Jesus's feet and learns, before Jesus specifically affirms Mary's choice (Luke 10:38–42). Most significantly, it describes Jesus himself, when he explains to his disciples that "whoever would be great among you must be your servant, and whoever would be first among you must be slave of all. For even the Son of Man came not to be served but to serve, and to give his life as a ransom for many" (Mark 10:43–45). Peter's mother-in-law's response to Jesus healing her is a model not just for women but for all of us. In Jesus's kingdom, serving isn't women's work. It's everybody's work.

How do we see Jesus through this self-giving woman's eyes? We see him as the one who takes us by the hand and lifts us up. We see him as the one whose touch can instantly relieve our pain, and as the one who serves us first before we even have the power to serve him. In 1662, the Anglican Book of Common Prayer described God as the one "whose service is perfect freedom," and we see this modeled by Peter's mother-in-law. So often in our modern life, we see service and freedom as opposites. But Peter's mother-in-law, 2,000 years ago, knew what modern psychologists have only recently discovered. We humans thrive when serving with a grateful heart, while endlessly self-realizing "freedom" makes us miserable.[2]

In Matthew, Mark, and Luke, the healing of Peter's mother-in-law and the demon-possessed man triggers a wave of sick and possessed people being brought to Jesus. Matthew interprets what was going on:

> That evening they brought to him many who were oppressed by demons, and he cast out the spirits with a word and healed all who were sick. This was to fulfill what was spoken by the prophet Isaiah: "He took our illnesses and bore our diseases." (Matt. 8:16–17)

Here we see spiritual and physical healing going hand in hand and, ever keen to show us how his Lord fulfills the Hebrew Scriptures, Matthew ties Jesus's actions back to Old Testament prophecy. In context, the quotation reads,

---

2. For more on this point, see Rebecca McLaughlin, *Confronting Christianity: 12 Hard Questions for the World's Largest Religion* (Wheaton, IL: Crossway, 2019), 22–27.

Surely he has borne our griefs and carried our sorrows; yet we esteemed him stricken, smitten by God, and afflicted. But he was pierced for our transgressions; he was crushed for our iniquities; upon him was the chastisement that brought us peace, and with his wounds we are healed. (Isa. 53:4–5)

The Hebrew word translated "griefs" here also means "sicknesses," and the word translated "sorrows" can also mean "pain." Here, in Isaiah, we see the mysterious figure of God's servant (Isa. 52:13) taking the sickness, sin, and suffering of God's people on himself. When Jesus heals Peter's mother-in-law and goes on to heal many more from both physical and spiritual illnesses, he is taking on the role of the suffering servant.

Just as Jesus is sometimes painted as a great teacher of universal truths but not as the great God of all the universe, so people sometimes seek to separate Jesus's work of healing our sicknesses from his work of taking the punishment for our sin. But Matthew does not let us drive this wedge. When Jesus died on the cross, he took the punishment for all our sin. But he also burst open the door to God's coming new creation, where there will be no more death or mourning or crying or pain (Rev. 21:4). We still live with sin and sickness here and now. But if we're followers of Jesus, we're peeking through a keyhole into a whole new, different world, where sin and suffering will be banished everlastingly by Jesus and his resurrection life. Jesus didn't come only to give his life *for* us. He also came to share his life *with* us. When Jesus heals

Peter's mother-in-law, she gets a tiny foretaste of his resurrection life, and she immediately uses it to serve.

WIDOW OF NAIN

When C. S. Lewis lost his wife to cancer, he wrote a reflection on death wrought of his messy pain. It's a short book with an almost clinical title—*A Grief Observed*—and it's one of the most powerful pieces of writing I've ever read. The passage that most frequently haunts me is this:

> I look up at the night sky. Is anything more certain than that in all those vast times and spaces, if I were allowed to search them, I should nowhere find her face, her voice, her touch? She died. She is dead. Is the word so difficult to learn?[3]

Lewis had pleaded with God for his wife, Joy. He'd married her when he knew she was dying. In fact, her cancer diagnosis had jolted him into the realization that he loved her. They were both followers of Jesus, but her peace about her death was so much greater than his. He feared her leaving him so desperately. He prayed so hard for God to end her suffering with healing, not with death. At first, Joy experienced remission. But then the cancer came back. God's answer to Lewis's fervent prayer was no.

3.   C. S. Lewis, *A Grief Observed* (London: Faber and Faber, 1966), 15.

Time and again in the Gospels, people plead with Jesus for healing. As we saw in chapter 2, when Jesus heals Lazarus, he doesn't respond to Mary and Martha's plea at first. As we saw in chapter 3, when the Syrophoenician woman prays for her daughter's healing—"Lord, help me!"—Jesus, at first, doesn't answer her prayer. In both cases, he works in the waiting with the women who are pleading for his help. He builds relationships in the space between their call and his response. For some of us, like Lazarus, we'll enter death before the Great Physician comes to heal our bodies. But sometimes, Jesus comes to us before we've even asked.

Luke tells a story where Jesus heads to the town of Nain in Galilee, followed by a massive crowd. As he approaches the gate of the town, "a man who had died was being carried out, the only son of his mother, and she was a widow" (Luke 7:12). A large crowd was coming with her to mourn her son. Then Luke writes,

> And when the Lord saw her, he had compassion on her and said to her, "Do not weep." Then he came up and touched the bier, and the bearers stood still. And he said, "Young man, I say to you, arise." And the dead man sat up and began to speak, and Jesus gave him to his mother. (vv. 13–15)

This is the first time Luke as narrator uses the term "the Lord" to refer to Jesus. What does Jesus do with his authority? He has compassion on a widow.

In the Old Testament, the Lord's compassion for the vulnerable—especially for widows, orphans, and refugees—is deeply embedded in his identity. For instance, Moses declares to God's people,

> The LORD your God is God of gods and Lord of lords, the great, the mighty, and the awesome God, who is not partial and takes no bribe. He executes justice for the fatherless and the widow, and loves the sojourner, giving him food and clothing. (Deut. 10:17–18)

Likewise, David calls God, "Father of the fatherless and protector of widows" (Ps. 68:5). God's law was filled with orders to provide for and protect widows and orphans, and abusing them came with a stern warning from the Lord: "You shall not mistreat any widow or fatherless child. If you do mistreat them, and they cry out to me, I will surely hear their cry, and my wrath will burn, and I will kill you with the sword, and your wives shall become widows and your children fatherless" (Ex. 22:22–24). The Lord Jesus's compassion for the bereaved widow, as she follows the corpse of her son out of Nain, is perfectly aligned with the character of God.

This woman has no husband and now her only son has died as well. This likely will leave her without income. On top of her grief, she may face destitution. But Jesus tells her not to weep, and then he calls her dead son back to life. Just as John calls Lazarus "the man who had died" (John 11:44), so Luke calls this widow's son "the dead man" to underline his utter lifelessness. But then, on Jesus's command, he sits up and begins to speak (Luke 7:15). Luke highlights once again the care that Jesus shows for this lamenting widow when he writes, "Jesus gave him to his mother" (v. 15).

How do we see Jesus through this widow's eyes? We see him as the one who comes to us before we've even asked and has compassion. We see him as the one who meets us in our desperate grief and shows his power to raise the dead. Just as he told this woman not to weep, so Jesus will one day wipe every tear from our eyes, if we will only trust in him (Rev. 21:4). The last English words of Lewis's *A Grief Observed* describe his wife Joy as she died: "She smiled. But not at me."[4] The Bible doesn't promise us that Jesus will always heal our loved ones when we ask. In fact, we can expect the heartache of the separation Lewis dreaded to invade our lives. But it does promise us that Jesus will be with us in our pain, and that one day he'll speak life into the dead, just as he spoke life into this broken widow's son.

BLEEDING WOMAN AND A DYING GIRL

"Do you know the song, 'Touch the Hem of his Garment'?" The question came from a Jewish friend. It's by soul music pioneer Sam Cooke, and she told me she'd played it to her daughter at bedtime for the first two years of her life. I'd never heard the song. But when I looked it up, I saw why it moved her. It's based on one of

4.   Lewis, *Grief Observed*, 64.

the most heart-grabbing stories told in any of the Gospels: the story of a bleeding woman who touched the hem of Jesus's garments. It's told by Matthew, Mark, and Luke. We don't know this woman's name. But her story has left its imprint on the world to such an extent that 2,000 years later, my Jewish friend was moved to use it as a lullaby. When we read it in context, the story becomes yet more arresting, as it's tied up with another miracle, in which a young girl is raised from the dead.

In Mark's account, a synagogue leader named Jairus falls at Jesus's feet and begs him earnestly, "My little daughter is at the point of death. Come and lay your hands on her, so that she may be made well and live" (Mark 5:22–23). Jesus goes with Jairus right away, and a great crowd goes with him. But the Gospel authors focus on one particular woman in the crush:

> And there was a woman who had had a discharge of blood for twelve years, and who had suffered much under many physicians, and had spent all that she had, and was no better but rather grew worse. She had heard the reports about Jesus and came up behind him in the crowd and touched his garment. For she said, "If I touch even his garments, I will be made well." (vv. 25–28)

Seldom do the Gospels include internal monologue. When they do, it's usually a peek inside the minds of the Pharisees, who are scandalized by Jesus, or the disciples, who tend to misunderstand him. But here we get a poignant glimpse of Jesus through this woman's eyes, as she says to herself, "If I touch even his garments, I will be made well" (cf. Matt. 9:21).

How do we see Jesus through this woman's eyes in this moment? We see him as the one she grasps at in her desperation, her final hope for healing, her last resort when her money is gone and her doctors have failed. But while we see her faith in Jesus's power, we also see her fear. Like men with bodily emissions, menstruating women were considered ceremonially unclean (see Lev. 15). Uncleanness was not sinful. It was unavoidable at times, both for men and for women, but it kept people from entering the temple. This woman's chronic condition would mean she's been unable to participate in temple worship for the last 12 years. Any contact with a bleeding woman would transfer the uncleanness. So, rather than asking Jesus for help, she comes up behind him and reaches for his clothing unawares. She's lived for 12 years with the shame of her condition, likely infertile and unable to participate in temple worship, and she's hoping to go unnoticed in the throng as she reaches out to Jesus.

This woman's desperate risk paid off: "immediately the flow of blood dried up, and she felt in her body that she was healed of her disease" (Mark 5:29). But in the same instant that she feels the blood stop flowing out of her, Jesus feels the power flowing out of him: "Jesus, perceiving in himself that power had gone out from him, immediately turned about in the crowd and said, 'Who touched my garments?'" (v. 30). Jesus's disciples point out the strangeness of his question: "You see the crowd pressing around you, and yet you say, 'Who touched me?'" (v. 31). But Jesus looks around to see who has done it. This turn of events is not what the woman had planned. "Knowing what had happened to her," Mark writes, she "came in fear and trembling and fell down before him and told him the whole truth" (v. 33). Given her condition, the woman is doubtless afraid she'll be rebuked for touching Jesus. But instead of condemnation, Jesus offers affirmation: "Daughter, your faith has made you well; go in peace, and be healed of your disease" (v. 34).

The first Jewish readers of the Gospels would have seen the woman's ceremonial uncleanness as central to the story. For most of us , that aspect may seem irrelevant. But the way Jesus receives this bleeding woman shows he doesn't shy away from the physicality of femaleness. Even the normal experience of menstruation can be grueling. For many women, periods come with physical discomfort and emotional distress. For some, the pain is debilitating. I don't know if you're male or female, or how comfortable or uncomfortable this paragraph is making you. Maybe you're a woman reading this, and you dread bleeding every month. Maybe you're struggling with infertility, and every period reminds you there is no baby hidden away in your womb. Perhaps your heart is twinging with lament because you have suffered miscarriage: blood one day announced the death of your newly beloved. Or maybe you're lurching into menopause or looking back on it with mixed feelings about the loss of periods. Even if you've suffered little menstrual pain, I doubt you relish bleeding every month. For most women, it feels like a side effect of femaleness that the advertising disclaimer would race through while the marketers distract us with footage of a woman skipping slo-mo through a field!

But Jesus does not recoil. Instead, he welcomes this woman who has bled for 12 years straight as a daughter filled with faith. He gives her peace. Strikingly, this woman is the only individual in all the Gospels whom Jesus calls "daughter" (Matt. 9:22; Mark 5:34; Luke 8:48). The woman who dared not come to him directly, but touched his clothing secretly, is recognized by Jesus intimately. She's his daughter. Of course she has the right to touch him.

This story whispers down the centuries to us that the aspect of femaleness women work hardest to hide is not repulsive to our Savior. He made me as a woman with a womb that sheds its lining every month, unless it's establishing a home for a new human in his image. Any shame we women feel around the physical realities of femaleness must melt away at Jesus's words. The one who has numbered the hairs on our heads also knows every drop of blood in our bodies. Instead of humiliating this woman, Jesus validates her. She's been excluded from the temple for 12 years, and now she's welcomed by the one who *is* the temple where we meet with God (John 2:18–22). If we come to Jesus with our need, our desperation, and our shame, we can know he will receive us with tenderness too. He may not heal us here and now. He doesn't promise that. But when we come to him in need, he surely turns himself toward us and receives us, just as he received this woman's touch and justified her actions: "Daughter, your faith has made you well" (Mark 5:34).

Jesus's words to this woman feel like a happy ending. But suddenly we are jolted back to Jairus's story. Mark tells us that while Jesus was still speaking, people come from Jairus's house and say, "Your daughter is dead. Why trouble the Teacher any further?" (v. 35). It's a crushing blow, and it intensifies the criticism the bleeding woman might receive. She's delayed Jesus on an urgent mission. Couldn't she have waited to have her chronic condition healed until after Jesus had saved the life of a dying child? But Jesus shows no hint of regret. He says to Jairus, "Do not fear, only believe" (v. 36), and, breaking off from the crowd with only Peter, James, and John, he goes to Jairus's house.

When they arrive at Jairus's house, many people are there, mourning for the girl. But Jesus says, "Why are you making a commotion and weeping? The child is not dead but sleeping" (vv. 38–39). In contrast to Jairus and to the bleeding woman, these people don't have faith in Jesus. Instead, they laugh at him. So, Jesus sends them out; takes the child's father and mother and Peter, James, and John; and goes to the room where the girl is lying dead. The scene Mark paints is intimate. Jesus shuts the crowd out as he enters into this family's grief. We get a rare snatch of Aramaic, their shared mother tongue. Taking her by the hand, Jesus says to the girl, "Talitha cumi," which means, "Little girl, I say to you, arise" (vv. 40–41).

Luke tells us at the beginning of the story that this girl is 12 years old (Luke 8:42). Mark saves that detail for the end (Mark 5:42). She had been alive as long as the bleeding woman had been sick. The girl was hitting puberty. The woman's life had been ruined by malfunctioning menstruation. Under Old Testament law, just as Jesus would be made ceremonially unclean by contact with a bleeding woman, so he would be made unclean by touching a dead body. But Jesus is no more put off by our inevitable uncleanness than a mother who has just given birth would be put off from holding her blood-smeared newborn. Before long, Jesus would bleed for this woman and die for this girl. But in this moment, he just makes them well. Mark tells us that "immediately the girl got up and began walking (for she was twelve years of age), and they were immediately overcome with amazement. And [Jesus] strictly charged them that no one should know this, and told them to give her something to eat" (vv. 42–43).

How do we see Jesus through this 12-year-old girl's eyes? We see him as we'll each see Jesus one day, if we put our trust in him. When Jesus calls us out of death and into everlasting life with him, we'll see him for the first time face-to-face. Jesus tells this girl's parents to give her something to eat. But when he calls our long-dismembered bodies back to life, he'll be the master of a feast that will continue to eternity. Jesus doesn't raise this girl from death to life for show. He does it because he cares. And one day, likely when our bodies have eroded and our names have been erased, Jesus will call us back to life with the same power and tenderness he showed the bleeding woman and the dead little girl.

DAUGHTER OF ABRAHAM

Growing up, I remember that my dad would sometimes have tears in his eyes just looking at me. I didn't understand. Now I have two daughters of my own, and I do. My girls are just so precious to me. If you could get sick from your mother telling you too often that she loves you, they'd be ruined. "Daughter" is a beautiful word. As we just saw, Jesus acknowledges the bleeding woman who touched his garment as his daughter while on the way to heal Jairus's daughter. The last healing miracle involving a woman in Luke also features a synagogue ruler and Jesus acknowledging a daughter. But the setup could not be more different. Jairus kneels down before Jesus and begs him to heal the daughter he loves. But the synagogue ruler in this story—who ought to have cared for a suffering daughter of Abraham—instead complains when Jesus heals her.

Jesus is teaching in a synagogue on the Sabbath, and "there was a woman who had had a disabling spirit for eighteen years," Luke records. "She was bent over and could not fully straighten herself" (Luke 13:11). The woman's condition is attributed to "a disabling spirit," but there's no indication that she is demon-possessed. The sense is more that Satan is responsible for her condition. Luke tells us that "when Jesus saw her, he called her over to him and said, 'Woman, you are freed from your disability.' And he laid his hands on her, and immediately she was made straight, and she glorified God" (vv. 12–13).

The bleeding woman came up to Jesus on her own accord. But Jesus calls this disabled woman to himself. Perhaps she'd heard that Jesus was in town, and she'd come with hopes of healing. Or maybe this was just her hometown synagogue, and she was there that Sabbath day to worship God as usual. We don't know her whole story. But we see Jesus through her eyes as one who, with his words and hands, can free us from our suffering. In an instant, an 18-years-long chain of pain was broken. While many come to Jesus in the Gospels and bow down, this woman finally stands up and glorifies God. But Jesus isn't finished with her yet.

Instead of celebrating with this woman, the synagogue ruler is angry. He says to the people, "There are six days in which work ought to be done. Come on those days and be healed, and not on the Sabbath day" (v. 14). This room-chilling reaction recalls the Pharisees' response to Jesus healing a man with a withered hand in Luke 6. That healing also takes place in a synagogue on the Sabbath, and the Pharisees are specifically watching to see if Jesus will heal on the Sabbath so that they can find a reason to accuse him. When Jesus heals the man, they are "filled with fury and [discuss] with one another what they might do to Jesus" (Luke 6:11). Like the Pharisees, the synagogue ruler does not attack Jesus directly. Instead, he launches a covert attack on the woman for coming on the Sabbath to be healed—despite the fact that Jesus had initiated the healing.

Having stood the disabled woman up straight for the first time in 18 years, Jesus then stands up for her:

Then the Lord answered him, "You hypocrites! Does not each of you on the Sabbath untie his ox or his donkey from the manger and lead it away to water it? And ought not this woman, a daughter of Abraham whom Satan bound for eighteen years, be loosed from this bond on the Sabbath day?" (Luke 13:15–16)

The expression "a daughter of Abraham" is unique in all the Bible. Jesus uses a parallel expression later in Luke, when he says of a repentant tax collector named Zacchaeus, "he also is a son of Abraham" (Luke 19:9). But the assertion that this woman is a *daughter* of Abraham is remarkable. This woman is an heir to God's promises to Abraham—the founding father of the Jews—as much as any Jewish man. Her response of praise to God sharply contrasts with the synagogue ruler's reaction and shows that she is a true heir of Abraham, while he is not. Luke ends the story by dividing the audience in two, those who followed the synagogue ruler in their critique and those who followed the woman in her praise: "As he said these things, all his adversaries were put to shame, and all the people rejoiced at all the glorious things that were done by him" (Luke 13:17). There is no neutral when it comes to Jesus. We can receive his words of life, or we can stand against him and be put to shame.

We don't know if this "daughter of Abraham" joins the healed women who travel around with Jesus. We don't know whether the woman who had bled for 12 years and was welcomed as his daughter comes with him. We don't know whether Jairus's daughter pleads with her parents for her family to hit the road with Jesus, or whether the widow of Nain takes up with him. Perhaps they do. Perhaps instead they sign on as disciples who stay in their hometown, like Mary and Martha. But through each of these women's eyes, we see Jesus as the one who brings healing to the sick, life to the dead, welcome to the outcasts, and honor to the scorned.

Through these healed women's eyes, we see Jesus as the one who can make us whole if we just touch the hem of his garment, but whose garments were divided up by lot and given to the soldiers who crucified him (Luke 23:34; Matt. 27:35). We see him as the one who came to bear our griefs and carry our sicknesses, the one who bled for us more painfully than the menstruating woman bled, the one who died for us more absolutely than the 12-year-old girl died, the one whose back was bent under the weight of a cruel cross so our backs could be straightened up one day, when he calls us from our graves and welcomes us as sons and daughters of Abraham.

My dying friend is ready to meet her Lord and praying for courage in the suffering to come. She is not lacking faith that Jesus will heal her. She's absolutely confident he will, because one day, he'll call her and her husband out of their graves to resurrection life with him, and they will be made whole.

DISCUSSION QUESTIONS

Getting Started: When you have a cold, what's your go-to comforting home remedy?

1. Why did each of the women in this chapter need healing? How did people respond to these healings?

2. How does Jesus's compassion for the widow of Nain reflect the heart of the Lord in the Old Testament?

3. How do Jesus's healings point ahead to something greater?

4. How do the healing stories in this chapter illustrate how Jesus fulfills Isaiah 53:4–5?

5. The dead son of the widow, the woman with the blood flow, and Jairus's dead daughter were all ceremonially unclean. Yet rather than becoming unclean himself, Jesus's touch makes them clean. How does this dynamic correlate to Jesus saving us from sin?

6. When have you or someone you know prayed to the Lord for healing? Did you see the healing you were hoping for?

7. Where are you longing for healing now? How can these healing stories give you hope, whether or not you receive the healing when and how you desire?

8. How do you see Jesus most meaningfully through the eyes of these women?

Going Deeper: Read Mark 5:25–34.

1. What do we know about the woman with the blood flow from the details provided in the text? What inferences might you draw about her social status and emotional state?

2. Why might the woman with blood flow have attempted to hide herself in the crowd of people to touch Jesus? See Leviticus 15:19–31 for help.

3. When did the woman's blood flow dry up (v. 29)? How did Jesus respond? Why do you think Jesus didn't let her slip away quietly?

FORGIVENESS

LAST NIGHT, I watched "Adele One Night Only." The British star performed at the Griffith Observatory in Los Angeles, both under the stars and with a star-infested audience, and the footage of her show was interspersed with an intimate interview with Oprah. Adele opened her performance with "Hello." As Oprah observed, the music video for that song has been watched 3 billion times. It frames the song as a lament for a broken relationship. The woman has called a thousand times to try to say sorry for breaking her loved one's heart. He's moved on, but she's stuck in her regret. It's a song of longing for forgiveness and lost love, of yearning for a locked door to be reopened. Perhaps we've all felt strains of this at times. Perhaps we've all longed for forgiveness and for once-discarded love.

In this chapter, we'll explore two stories of forgiveness for women who might well think they've gone too far to be brought back and welcomed in. We'll see how Jesus treats women who've been vilified as moral trash and how he uses their example to expose the moral failure of the men who judge them. We'll see how Jesus welcomes prostitutes into God's kingdom while the self-appointed gatekeepers look on in horror. We'll glimpse the radical forgiveness Jesus offers, even to those who are dragged into his presence, and see how the door to everlasting love with Jesus is wide open now—if we will only come to him.

PROSTITUTES IN THE KINGDOM

Last summer, I was driving with my children to the beach. As we were stopped in traffic, I noticed a woman who was going car-to-car ahead of us. She was evidently poor, but she wasn't begging, as several homeless people do at traffic lights on routes we often take. It took me a moment to realize what the strange, faux-joyful dance she was enacting as she weaved between the cars was meant to signal. I was not her target, but my heart went out to her. I wondered how her life had brought her to that moment, and I prayed that God would reach her with a love she'd never known before. She was clearly hoping to be picked up by a man who'd pay for her body. I hoped instead that she'd be picked up by the man who came to pay with his life for women just like her. You see, Jesus welcomed prostitutes: not like the other men of his day, and of ours, but like a loving brother, searching for his sister in the slums to bring her home.

They say that you know somewhere is your home when you have the right to rearrange the furniture. When Jesus was 12, he'd claimed the temple was his Father's house (Luke 2:49). When Jesus enters the temple as an adult, we see him rearrange the furniture in a dramatic way. Matthew tells us that he "drove out all who sold and bought in the temple, and he overturned the tables of the money-changers and the seats of those who sold pigeons" (Matt. 21:12). This rearrangement makes the chief priests and the scribes angry. They ask Jesus, "By what authority are you doing these things, and who gave you this authority?" (v. 23). As usual, Jesus doesn't answer them directly. First, he asks them what they think of John the Baptist, knowing this will put them in a bind, because he is so popular with the people. Then he tells a story to help them see their situation:

> What do you think? A man had two sons. And he went to the first and said, "Son, go and work in the vineyard today." And he answered, "I will not," but afterward he changed his mind and went. And he went to the other son and said the same. And he answered, "I go, sir," but did not go. Which of the two did the will of his father? (vv. 28–31)

The chief priests and the elders say, "The first." And Jesus says to them, "Truly, I say to you, the tax collectors and the prostitutes go into the kingdom of God before you. For John came to you in the way of righteousness, and you did not believe him, but the tax collectors and the prostitutes believed him. And even when you saw it, you did not afterward change your minds and believe him" (vv. 31–32).

Jesus's words are scandalous. The tax collectors and prostitutes were the apex of sinners from a Jewish point of view. Conversely, the chief priests and elders would have seen themselves at the top of the religious tree. But Jesus tells them bluntly that the Roman-sympathizing swindlers and the prostitutes—the very people they'd vilify—are entering God's kingdom ahead of them. Why? Because the prostitutes and tax collectors are repenting of their sin. Indeed, Jesus speaks as if the chief priests and the elders should be following their example.

Jesus's message is the same today. The woman weaving her way between the cars may well repent and enter Jesus's kingdom while the most respectable mother of four who volunteers on all the school committees and is married to an elder in a church does not. A man imprisoned for his crimes may well repent and enter Jesus's kingdom while a respectable police chief never does. The question for people wanting to enter is not, "Are you a sinner?" but "Have you repented?" Jesus offers free and full forgiveness for the prostitutes and tax collectors who will come to him. In fact, it seems they flocked to him while many of the most religious Jews refused to come.

Jesus's words concerning prostitutes are radical to a degree that's hard for us to grasp. His fellow Jews saw prostitutes as sinners to be avoided at all costs—and certainly not as people who might walk right into the kingdom of God. But in the wider Greco-Roman empire,

Jesus's comment was, if anything, even more disruptive, because Jesus is recognizing prostitutes as valid human beings in and of themselves.

In Rome, "men no more hesitated to use slaves and prostitutes to relieve themselves of their sexual needs than they did to use the side of a road as a toilet."[1] Sex with prostitutes was not seen as immoral, but as a legitimate and necessary outlet for male lust. Indeed, as historian Kyle Harper explains, "The sex industry was integral to the moral economy of the classical world."[2] But prostitutes themselves were seen as almost literally worthless. The average cost of sex with a prostitute was equal to the cost of a loaf of bread.[3] As Harper puts it, "The brutal exposure of vulnerable women rested on a public indifference so vast that it lay invisibly at the very foundations of the ancient sexual order."[4] Nobody cared about prostitutes beyond the services they could provide.

Jesus's teaching introduced two tectonic shifts. First, he loved and valued women—including prostitutes. Second, against the norms of the empire, he upheld faithful marriage as the only context for sex. This started a sexual revolution more daring than the revolution of the 1960s, but in the opposite direction.

---

1. Tom Holland, *Dominion: How the Christian Revolution Remade the World* (New York: Basic Books, 2019), 99.

2. Kyle Harper, *From Shame to Sin: The Christian Transformation of Sexual Morality in Late Antiquity* (Cambridge, MA: Harvard University Press), 3.

3. Harper, *Shame to Sin*, 49.

4. Harper, *Shame to Sin*, 15.

The modern sexual revolution offered women the right to commitment-free sex: a right that many men had been assuming over the centuries. But the sexual revolution that was triggered by the rise of Christianity within the Roman empire cut out men's sexual freedom and called them to the kind of faithfulness in marriage that had previously only been expected of wives. This meant that women could no longer be seen as expendable objects of male lust. Rather, sex only belonged in marriage—the permanent, God-given, one-flesh union of a man and a woman (Matt. 19:4–6)—and Christian husbands were to love their wives with the same kind of sacrificial love that Christ has for his church (Eph. 5:25). It's obvious why such a change would be good news for women who would previously have been the victims of coercive sex. But as we saw in the introduction, there is a growing body of evidence to suggest that commitment-free sex does measurable harm to women's happiness and health even when it is freely chosen. Jesus's sexual ethics truly lead to human flourishing. But while Jesus defined all sex outside of marriage as sinful (Mark 7:21), he also welcomed even the most notorious sexual sinners who put their trust in him.

How do we see Jesus through the eyes of these repentant prostitutes? We see him as the only man who welcomes them not for what he can get but for what he can give. We see him as the one who does not count their history against them, but who knows each detail of their past and welcomes them into his stunning future. We see him as a magnet for those who feel like scraps of human metal on life's junk heap, picking up the broken and abused and drawing them into his kingdom of love.

SINFUL WOMAN

We get further insight into Jesus's attitude toward women who were known as sinners from a striking story in Luke's Gospel. Right before telling us about Jesus's encounter with a notoriously sinful woman, Luke recounts Jesus reflecting on his own bad reputation. Jesus points out that sometimes you can't win. John the Baptist came "eating no bread and drinking no wine" and was accused of having a demon (Luke 7:33). Jesus comes "eating and drinking" and people say, "Look at him! A glutton and a drunkard, a friend of tax collectors and sinners" (v. 34). What Jesus does next makes his reputation even worse.

Jesus has been invited to dinner at the house of one of the Pharisees. This is surprising, given how often Pharisees are confronting Jesus. Perhaps this Pharisee is giving Jesus a chance to redeem himself. But then something extremely embarrassing happens:

A woman of the city, who was a sinner, when she learned that [Jesus] was reclining at table in the Pharisee's house, brought an alabaster flask of ointment, and standing behind him at his feet, weeping, she began to wet his feet with her tears and wiped them with the hair of her head and kissed his feet and anointed them with the ointment. (vv. 37–38)

At special feasts, it was common for the guests to recline and for the doors to be left open. Folks who weren't invited could sit around the walls of the room, listen to the conversation, and perhaps get scraps of food. So, the entry of a nonofficial guest is not remarkable. But her identity and actions are. We don't know all the details of this woman's sin. She may have been a prostitute. She may have been known as a "sinner" in some other way. In any case, we see from Luke's description and the Pharisees' response that she's the kind of woman a Jewish rabbi should have shunned. But here she is, showing extravagant love to Jesus in the most self-humbling way, and Jesus is just letting her.

This woman's actions mirror the actions of Mary of Bethany, which we explored in chapter 2. Both women anoint Jesus's body with ointment from an alabaster jar while he is reclining at the table. Both wipe his feet with their hair. Both incidents happen in the house of someone named Simon: Simon the Pharisee versus Simon the Leper. Some have suggested that Luke is reporting on the same event as Matthew, Mark, and John. But Simon was the most common name among Jewish men of Jesus's time and place, and the contexts of the two stories are very different.[5] Unlike Mary of Bethany, this woman is portrayed as a notorious sinner. Rather than being criticized for wasting money as Mary was, this woman is seen as toxic in and of herself. The parallels aren't because

5. For the popularity of the name Simon/Simeon see Bauckham, *Jesus and the Eyewitnesses*, 85.

Luke is telling the same story as Matthew, Mark, and John, but because both these women knew that Jesus deserved the most extravagant love. And just as Mary was the disciple Judas Iscariot ought to have been, so this anonymous, sinful woman of the city shows the love that Simon the Pharisee should have shown.

Luke tells us how Simon reacts: "Now when the Pharisee who had invited [Jesus] saw this, he said to himself, 'If this man were a prophet, he would have known who and what sort of woman this is who is touching him, for she is a sinner'" (v. 39). From Simon's point of view, Jesus should know that contact with this sinful woman will contaminate him morally—like rolling in fast-spreading mold. In this moment, Simon the Pharisee is the opposite of the Samaritan woman we met in chapter 3. She recognized Jesus as a prophet when she found he knew about her sexual history. Simon thinks Jesus *cannot* be a prophet, because he must *not* realize who this sinful woman is. But Jesus knows exactly who she is. He knows who Simon is as well.

We don't know whether Simon speaks his critique under his breath or just in his head, but Jesus hears it either way. "Simon," he responds, "I have something to say to you." The Pharisee answers with at least feigned respect: "Say it, Teacher" (v. 40). So, Jesus tells a story like the one he'd told the chief priests and the elders when he broke the news that prostitutes were entering God's kingdom ahead of them:

A certain moneylender had two debtors. One owed five hundred denarii, and the other fifty. When they could not pay, he cancelled the debt of both. Now which of them will love him more? (vv. 41–42)

Five hundred denarii is a massive debt—equivalent to about 20 months of wages. Fifty is about two months' pay. Simon answers, "The one, I suppose, for whom he cancelled the larger debt." Jesus replies, "You have judged rightly." Then turning toward the woman, Jesus asks Simon, "Do you see this woman?" (vv. 43–44).

The fact is, Jesus and Simon both see the woman. But they see her very differently. Simon sees her as a sinner with no business touching Jesus's feet. He sees her as offensive, morally corrupt, deserving of scorn. Simon sees her as a litmus test: Jesus cannot be a prophet if he lets this woman touch him. But Jesus sees her as the one who does what Simon should have done. Indeed, Jesus goes on to make a point-by-point comparison between the morally respectable Pharisee and the morally bankrupt woman of the city:

I entered your house; you gave me no water for my feet, but she has wet my feet with her tears and wiped them with her hair. You gave me no kiss, but from the time I came in she has not ceased to kiss my feet. You did not anoint my head with oil, but she has anointed my feet with ointment. Therefore I tell you, her sins, which are many, are forgiven—for she loved much. But he who is forgiven little, loves little. (vv. 44–47)

Simon thinks that Jesus should be ashamed to be touched by this woman, that he should recoil from her like someone spitting rancid milk out of their mouth. But Jesus thinks that Simon is the one who ought to be ashamed. This sinful woman is doing all the things for Jesus that Simon failed to do. Why? Because she loves him.

How do we see Jesus through this woman's eyes at this moment? We see him as the source of her forgiveness and the object of her love. We see him as the one for whom it's worth humiliating herself before a crowd. We see him as the one for whom it's worth sacrificing both her money and her dignity, as she pours out expensive ointment on his feet and wipes them with her hair. Jesus is so far above her that she cannot abase herself enough in his presence. But through her eyes, we also see Jesus as the one who stands with sinners like her—and like you, and like me. As we've seen through the eyes of many women in this book so far, Jesus is the one who defends despised women against the censure of powerful men. And even as this sinful woman of the city bends down, we see Jesus lift her up as a shining, tear-stained paragon of love to humble the self-righteous Pharisee. But Jesus hasn't finished with her yet.

After his rebuke of Simon, Jesus turns to the woman again and says, "Your sins are forgiven" (v. 48). This statement causes a further stir. Luke tells us that "those who were at table with him began to say among themselves, 'Who is this, who even forgives sins?'" (v. 49). Only God has that right. Yet Jesus tells this woman that her sins are washed away, as surely as her tears have washed his feet.

Jesus is the moneylender, to whom both the Pharisee and the notorious woman owed a debt. Her extravagant love is the result of his extravagant forgiveness. Simon the Pharisee may think he has less debt to pay to God than this woman does. Jesus doesn't fight him on that. Instead, he shows him through this woman what a forgiven person looks like. Then Jesus says to her, "Your faith has saved you; go in peace" (v. 50).

We don't know whether this forgiven woman joined Jesus's traveling band of disciples or not. But right after telling this story, Luke tells us about the women—like Mary Magdalene, Joanna, and Susanna—who did (Luke 8:1–3). These women were ready to leave everything for Jesus. They had been healed and forgiven, and they followed him wherever he went. Jesus will take anyone. He took Mary Magdalene, from whom he had to cast out seven demons (v. 2). He took the sinful woman of the city, whose touch was seen as morally contaminating. He's taken me, and he'll take you. But anyone who thinks they only need a little bit of forgiveness from God will find themselves shut out of his kingdom—shoved aside by the prostitutes and tax collectors and sinners who are getting in ahead of them. Why? Because, unlike the sinful woman of the city, they won't throw themselves at Jesus's feet.

SHOULD THIS STORY BE IN THE BIBLE?

John ends his Gospel with these words: "Now there are also many other things that Jesus did. Were every one of them to be written, I suppose the world itself could not contain the books that would be written" (John 21:25). We're going to spend the rest of our time in this chapter looking at a passage in John's Gospel that likely did not make John's original cut, but which is perfectly aligned with what we see of Jesus in the rest of John, and in the other Gospels, as he relates to women. Before we look at the story itself, we're going to take a moment to think through what we should make of a text like this that may or may not have been original.

If you open up a Bible to John 8, it will likely have a note that says, "The earliest manuscripts do not include 7:53–8:11." If you, like me, believe that the Bible is the Word of God, you might find a note like this one disconcerting. If, on the other hand, you're skeptical about the Gospels as reliable testimony about Jesus, you might see a note like this as proof that they should not be taken to be God's Word to us about his Son. How can we make grandiose claims about the Bible as the revelation of a perfect and all-powerful God if we're not sure that some parts of the texts are even original? We don't have the first physical manuscripts (known as autographs) that Matthew, Mark, Luke, and John wrote down. We have at best copies of their originals, and in many instances, our earliest manuscripts are likely copies of copies.[6] So, how do we know they didn't get corrupted in the

6. For a very helpful, accessible discussion of this see William D. Mounce, *Why I Trust the Bible: Answers to Real Questions and Doubts People Have About the Bible* (Grand Rapids, MI: Zondervan, 2021), 131–132.

process—pieces added here, subtracted there, or modified to suit the copyist's purposes?

Last week, I gave my daughter Miranda a Shakespeare exam. I've been teaching her and one of her middle school friends Shakespeare every Tuesday. As part of the course, I had them memorize four sonnets and a soliloquy. When I came to grade their papers, I noticed a small mistake in one of the sonnets in Miranda's manuscript. I then noticed the same mistake in her friend's. I looked the passage up to check I hadn't misremembered it myself. But no, it was their shared mistake. It turned out that Miranda had been helping her friend learn at school, so the small mistake Miranda made had been passed on. If I'd taught the same speeches to my best friend's kids in London, via Skype, they may have made mistakes as well. So, if we compared the papers from London and from Miranda and her friend here in Cambridge, Massachusetts, we'd see the passages that were in doubt. If I had also taught the children of my friends who live in San Francisco, Sydney, and Malawi, we could gather all the papers together and use them to correct each other. Each manuscript might have mistakes, but it's highly unlikely that five copies made independently would feature the same mistakes. The same is true for the biblical manuscripts due to the rapid, messy spread of Christianity. As Richard Bauckham explains, "[Jesus] lived in the Middle East, and in the first few centuries of Christianity the faith spread in all directions—not only to Greece and Rome, France and Spain, but also to Egypt, North Africa, and Ethiopia, to Turkey and Armenia, to Iraq, Persia, and India."[7] As the good news about Jesus caught on, the Gospel accounts of his life were eagerly copied and distributed. If we only had one copy of each Gospel, and we knew that it was a copy of a copy of a copy, we wouldn't know what errors had crept in along the way. Because we have thousands of copies of all or parts of the Gospels from a range of different places, we can compare copies made in one place with copies made independently in another and identify mistakes. The wealth of manuscripts from different places means that the vast majority of the Gospel texts we have in our Bibles today are not in question. But some are.

The last two lines of the Shakespeare sonnet my daughter was learning read, "So long as men can breathe or eyes can see, / So long lives this, and this gives life to thee."[8] She had written, "So long as men can breathe *and* eyes can see"—a change that makes almost no difference to the meaning of the line. The vast majority of the question marks over verses in the Gospels are like this: minor differences that make no substantial difference to the meaning of the text. But there are a handful of places where it's genuinely hard to tell what the originals said. When that happens, our modern Bibles make a note of it. One of the longest passages included in our Bibles

7. Richard Bauckham, *Jesus: A Very Short Introduction* (Oxford: Oxford University Press, 2011), 1.
8. William Shakespeare, "Shall I Compare Thee to a Summer's Day?" Poetry Foundation, accessed February 4, 2022, https://www.poetryfoundation.org/poems/45087/sonnet-18-shall-i-compare-thee-to-a-summers-day.

that comes with such a note is the story of a woman caught in adultery.

The earliest copies of John's Gospel that we have do not include this story. Some copies have it in different places in the text, and it's sometimes found in Luke's Gospel instead. One explanation is that this story was not in the original book that John wrote, but that it was passed down orally and later included in John because it so clearly deserved to be remembered. Nothing that Christians believe about Jesus stands or falls on this text. But its portrayal of Jesus is utterly consistent with the picture that the Gospel authors paint.

WOMAN CAUGHT IN ADULTERY

At the start of the story, Jesus is teaching in the temple. He'd caused a massive stir the previous day, and the chief priests and the Pharisees sent officers to arrest him. But the officers had been thrown off by their attraction to Jesus's teaching, "No one ever spoke like this man!" they report (John 7:46). This only made the Pharisees angrier. One Jewish leader named Nicodemus, whose nighttime visit to Jesus was recorded in John 3, stood up for Jesus without much success. But despite the heightened risk, Jesus has come back early in the morning the next day, and "all the people came to him, and he sat down and taught them" (John 8:2).

The scribes and the Pharisees were looking for a reason to get Jesus arrested, so they brought in a woman who had been caught in adultery, "and placing her in the midst," they said to Jesus, "Teacher, this woman has been caught in the act of adultery. Now in the Law, Moses commanded us to stone such women. So what do you say?" (vv. 4–5).

The tension in the scene is high. The command, "Do not commit adultery" was the seventh of the famous Ten Commandments God gave Moses after rescuing his people from slavery in Egypt (Ex. 20:14). What's more, the Old Testament law stated that if a man and a woman were caught in adultery, they should both be executed (Deut. 22:22; Lev. 20:10). Notably, the religious leaders haven't brought the man in question. They seem more keen to judge the woman. But they're most keen to judge Jesus. As John explains: "This they said to test him, that they might have some charge to bring against him" (John 8:6). If Jesus lets this woman off, he'll be going against the Jewish law. But if he affirms that she should be stoned, he risks falling foul of the Romans, who saw themselves as the legal authorities when it came to the execution of their Jewish subjects. Jesus has no motivation to avoid arrest. He knows he's headed for the cross. But he takes the opportunity to teach the people and to protect the woman.

Before giving any answer to the scribes and Pharisees, Jesus "bent down and wrote with his finger on the ground" (v. 6). We don't know exactly what this signifies. Various theories have been suggested. Maybe Jesus is writing the verdict on the ground. Maybe he is evoking the test of an unfaithful wife prescribed in the Old Testament, when dust from the floor of the tabernacle (the forerunner to the temple) was mixed with water for the woman to drink as a means of God judging or acquitting her (Num. 5:11–29). Maybe Jesus is just showing them how unafraid he is of anything the scribes and Pharisees could do to him. But they keep asking him what they should do.

Eventually, Jesus stands up and says, "Let him who is without sin among you be the first to throw a stone at her" (John 8:7). Then he goes back to writing on the ground. When the scribes and Pharisees hear his words, "they [go] away one by one, beginning with the older ones, and Jesus [is] left alone with the woman standing before him" (v. 9). When Jesus finally stands up again, he says, "Woman, where are they? Has no one condemned you?" She replies, "No one, Lord" (v. 10). This is the third time Jesus has addressed someone as "woman" in John. The first was his mother, at the wedding in Cana (John 2:4). The second was the Samaritan woman at the well (John 4:21). It's not a contemptuous term. Then Jesus says to this woman, caught in adultery, humiliated, and afraid for her life, "Neither do I condemn you; go, and from now on sin no more" (John 8:11).

How do we see Jesus through this woman's eyes? We see him as the one man with the right to judge her, but who chose instead to let her go. We see him as the one who forgave her sin and saved her life. We see him as the one who showed that she was not in a different category from the self-righteous religious leaders, but that every single person standing there was guilty of sexual sin—except Jesus himself.

Some people think this story lifts the weight off sexual sin. It doesn't. Jesus took adultery extremely seriously. But rather than only looking at the actions, he looked also at the heart. In his famous Sermon on the Mount in Matthew's Gospel, Jesus declared,

> You have heard that it was said, "You shall not commit adultery." But I say to you that everyone who looks at a woman with lustful intent has already committed adultery with her in his heart. (Matt. 5:27–28)

Jesus doesn't loosen the law when it comes to adultery, he tightens it. According to Jesus, sexual sin is more serious than a heart attack. He goes on:

> If your right eye causes you to sin, tear it out and throw it away. For it is better that you lose one of your members than that your whole body be thrown into hell. And if your right hand causes you to sin, cut it off and throw it away. For it is better that you lose one of your members than that your whole body go into hell. (vv. 29–30)

But rather than the dividing line being between the woman who was caught in the act of adultery and the men who were ready to stone her, Jesus applies this principle and draws a dividing line that places both the adulterous woman and also her accusers on the wrong side of the law. Jesus alone has the right to condemn her, but instead he forgives.

The video of Adele's song "Hello" tells a visual story of a broken romantic relationship that seems to match the lyrics of the song. But in interviews, Adele has said that the song is really about her getting over her sense of guilt and reconnecting with everyone—especially herself. In the 21st-century West, we tend to see guilt as an unhealthy feeling to be shed, and forgiving ourselves as more important than seeking forgiveness from others. But Jesus does not minimize our guilt. He takes it from us. We talk today about forgiving ourselves and learning to love ourselves. But if that's our focus, we risk missing out on the forgiveness and the love that Jesus offers us. It's not too late for us to say we're sorry. We don't have to call him a thousand times. He welcomes us with open arms.

DISCUSSION QUESTIONS

Getting Started: As a child, were you a rule follower or a rebel? Share an example from when you were young.

1. How did people in New Testament times view prostitutes?
2. What similarities and differences do you see between the story of Mary of Bethany anointing Jesus and the sinful woman anointing Jesus? How does this comparison provide a fuller picture of who Jesus is?
3. Read 1 Peter 2:22. In light of this verse, what is ironic about Jesus saying "let him who is without

sin among you be the first to throw a stone at her" in John 8:7?

4. What similarities do you notice in the ways Jesus responds to each of the sinful women in this chapter?

5. Who do you view as morally too far gone or outside the reach of God's kingdom? How does Jesus confront that belief?

6. Do you tend to compare your sin with the sins of others? Does that comparison give you false assurance that your sin isn't too bad, or lead you to despair because of the depth of your sin?

7. How do the stories of forgiveness in this chapter influence the way you respond to your own sin?

8. How do you see Jesus most meaningfully through the eyes of these women?

Going Deeper: Read Luke 7:36–50.

1. List the ways the sinful woman touches Jesus. How does Jesus break expectations with his response?

2. In what ways is the sinful woman contrasted with Simon the Pharisee? What does this juxtaposition reveal about what it means to love and serve Jesus?

3. What claim was Jesus making about himself when he told the woman her sins were forgiven (see Mark 2:7)?

CHAPTER 6

LIFE

THE LAST FILM my husband and I watched together is called *Red Notice*. It's a silly, funny action movie about art thieves trying to steal three bejeweled eggs that the Roman general Mark Antony supposedly gave to Cleopatra 2,000 years ago. Early in the film, one of the main characters (played by Dwayne Johnson, a.k.a. "The Rock") alerts an art museum in Rome that the egg on display there may have just been stolen. The museum director doesn't believe him. When they arrive in the display room, the egg looks present and correct. But Johnson uses a thermal sensor to show that it's not giving off the right radiation. The director says it's probably just an error in the sensor. So, Johnson takes a Coke from a small boy and pours it on the supposedly invaluable metalwork from antiquity. The egg disintegrates.

Without the bodily resurrection of Jesus, the Christian faith lies as dead and entombed as Jesus's corpse on that first Saturday. The wild claim first heard by his mother

Mary, that Jesus is God's everlasting King, falls flat on its face. There is no truth or hope or life in Christianity if Jesus was not raised. Some scholars, like Bart Ehrman, argue that when we examine the four Gospel accounts of Jesus's death and resurrection, the resurrection claim disintegrates before our eyes, like the Coke-baptized egg. But as we'll see in this chapter, if we look more closely at the Gospel passages, we find the opposite: not evidence of a fake, but signs of authenticity. One of these signs is that all four Gospels invite us to see Jesus's death and resurrection through the eyes of women.

WOMB TO TOMB

One bedtime, when my daughter Eliza was 5, she put her arms around my neck and asked, "Mummy, will you hold me when I'm dying?" "Yes, darling," I replied. Thank God, it's much more likely she'll hold me in death. Watching your child die is a horrifying prospect. If—God forbid—she should die first, I hope to hold her in my arms. But even if she dies in old age, when I'm long gone, Eliza may yet call for me. I recently learned that elderly people often cry out for their mothers when they're dying, retreating to a childlike need for comfort.

When he was on the point of death, Jesus called out to his mother too. But not so she could care for him. Rather, he cried out to care for her. John writes:

> When Jesus saw his mother and the disciple whom he loved standing nearby, he said to his mother,

"Woman, behold, your son!" Then he said to the disciple, "Behold, your mother!" And from that hour, the
disciple took her into his own home. (John 19:26–27)

The disciple whom Jesus loved is John's way of referring
to himself. We know that Jesus's half-brother James became a leader in the early church. But during his life on
earth, his biological siblings did not seem to grasp his
mission. Perhaps this is why Jesus entrusts his mother to
a beloved disciple's care. Just as he cared for the widow of
Nain, so he cares for his own mother. Mary was the first
to know who Jesus is. She cared for him in infancy. But
as Mary looks up at her son upon the cross—enduring
unimaginable agony—she finds what we will all find if
we will lift our eyes to him: that Jesus is the one who
truly cares for us.

OTHER WOMEN AT THE CROSS

It's hard for us to wrap our minds around what crucifixion meant in the first century. In his 2019 masterpiece,
*Dominion: How the Christian Revolution Remade the
World*, British historian Tom Holland attempts to help
us understand. It was "the worst death imaginable"—a
punishment designed for slaves to maximize their tor-
ture and humiliation. "So foul was the carrion-reek of
their disgrace," Holland explains, "that many felt tainted
even by viewing a crucifixion."[1] And yet all four New

1. Holland, *Dominion*, 2.

Testament Gospels highlight the women who deliberately chose to view Jesus's death.

In Jewish law, two or three witnesses were required when someone was charged with a crime (Deut. 19:15). This principle spilled over into other areas of life, so Matthew, Mark, and John all name three women in particular who watched the crucifixion.[2] Mark reports:

> There were also women looking on from a distance, among whom were Mary Magdalene, and Mary the mother of James the younger and of Joses, and Salome. When he was in Galilee, they followed him and ministered to him, and there were also many other women who came up with him to Jerusalem. (Mark 15:40–41)

As we will see, Mary Magdalene plays a central role across the Gospels as they testify to Jesus's resurrection. Matthew, Mark, and John all name her at the crucifixion too. Mark's second witness is another Mary, whose sons James and Joses (a variant spelling of Joseph) were likely well known to the early church.[3] Third, Mark cites a woman named Salome. Salome was the second most common

2. Bauckham, *Jesus and the Eyewitnesses*, 49.
3. Similarly, Baukham argues that Simon of Cyrene, whom Mark names earlier in his narrative as the one who was hauled in to carry Jesus's cross, is called "the father of Alexander and Rufus" (Mark 15:21), likely because his sons were known in the early church and Mark is appealing to their testimony concerning what their father saw. See Bauckham, *Jesus and the Eyewitnesses*, 52.

name among Jewish women of that time and place.[4] But Salome's name stands alone, suggesting that Mark's first readers would've heard of her and that there wasn't another Salome among Jesus's well-known disciples.

Matthew cites the same two women first as Mark. But instead of Salome, his third eyewitness is "the mother of the sons of Zebedee" (Matt. 27:56). As we saw in chapter 3, this woman is unique to Matthew and her presence at the cross redeems her misguided attempt to get her sons top spots in Jesus's kingdom. Luke—who introduced Mary Magdalene, Joanna, and Susanna as being among the many women who followed Jesus much earlier in his Gospel—simply tells us that "the women who had followed him from Galilee stood at a distance watching these things" (Luke 23:49). These women all knew Jesus intimately. They'd followed him for years. When he'd gone through cities and villages proclaiming the kingdom of God, they'd been with him. They'd seen him heal and teach and cast out demons. Now, they saw him nailed to a cross: eviscerated in the public gaze.

John is the only Gospel author who claims to have witnessed Jesus's crucifixion himself. But, like Matthew and Mark, he also records three female witnesses—all named Mary: "Standing by the cross of Jesus were his mother and his mother's sister, Mary the wife of Clopas, and Mary Magdalene" (John 19:25). Unlike the other two Marys on John's list, Mary the wife of Clopas is not

4. Bauckham, *Jesus and the Eyewitnesses*, 85.

a household name for us.[5] But early Christian writings reference a couple named Mary and Clopas (which was an uncommon name) as parents of a man named Simon, who was a key leader in the early church. Clopas was a brother of Jesus's adoptive father, Joseph, hence why John calls his wife, Mary, Jesus's mother's sister. So, this Mary would likely have been known to John's first audience as well.[6]

How do we see Jesus through the eyes of the many women who watched him being crucified—some who had been with him since Galilee and ministered to him, some who had come up with him to Jerusalem? We see him as the one they love, broken and mutilated, mocked, and despised. We see the sign above his head that read, "This is Jesus, King of the Jews" (Matt. 27:37). We see the one on whom all their God-sent faith was pinned now nailed to a Roman cross. We see him through their tears. But vitally, we see him.

For most of this book, as we have looked through women's eyes, we've seen Jesus as a hero. We've seen him as a teacher and a healer and a long-awaited King—as one who calls dead people from their graves and speaks divine forgiveness over sinners. But here we see him as

5. In the original Greek, the other woman John mentions is simply named "Mary of Clopas," but "the wife of" is likely implied.
6. Richard Bauckham argues that the Clopas referenced here by John is the same person as the Cleopas whom Luke names as one of two disciples who met the risen Jesus on the road to Emmaus (Luke 24:18), Cleopas being the Greek version of the Hebrew name. See Bauckham, *Gospel Women*, 208–9.

the one who suffered horrifying torment and excruciating death. We see him as a victim of the power of Rome. We see him in this moment not as universal Lord, but as a seeming failure. For us to see who Jesus really is, it's vital that we gaze at him upon the cross, as Mary Magdalene, and Mary the wife of Clopas, and Mary the mother of James and Joses, and his own mother Mary, and Salome and the mother of the sons of Zebedee all saw him on that day. But the women's role as witnesses did not end there. We must keep looking through their eyes.

WITNESSES OF JESUS'S BURIAL

It's easy to pass over Jesus's burial like an unimportant foothill between two great peaks. But the Gospel authors take time to document its witnesses. Once again, multiple women are named. This is especially remarkable as all four Gospel authors also cite a far more impressive witness at this point. Mark tells us that "Joseph of Arimathea, a respected member of the council, who was also himself looking for the kingdom of God, took courage and went to Pilate and asked for the body of Jesus" (Mark 15:43). Having been granted the corpse, "Joseph bought a linen shroud, and taking [Jesus] down, wrapped him in the linen shroud and laid him in a tomb that had been cut out of the rock" (v. 46). John's Gospel adds a second male witness at this point: a leader of the Pharisees named Nicodemus (John 19:39), whose story of visiting Jesus by night is narrated earlier (John 3:1–15). The testimony of these powerful men would've carried much more weight than that of Jesus's female followers. But Matthew, Mark, and Luke all point to the women who are there when Jesus is buried. It's vital that the women are familiar with Jesus's tomb, or else the force of them finding it empty on that first Easter morning will be lost.

Mark tells us that "Mary Magdalene and Mary the mother of Joses saw where [Jesus] was laid" (Mark 15:47). Likewise, Matthew tells us that when the entrance to Jesus's tomb is sealed with a rock, Mary Magdalene and the other Mary (i.e., Mary the mother of James and Joseph) were there, sitting opposite the tomb (Matt. 27:61). Notably, both Matthew and Mark leave out the third named witness from their crucifixion narratives when it comes to Jesus's burial, presumably because Susanna and the mother of the sons of Zebedee were not present. Matthew also tells us that a guard was set on Jesus's tomb to make it doubly secure (vv. 62–66). Again, Luke is more general, but he is nonetheless keen for us to know that Jesus's female disciples watched his burial: "The women who had come with him from Galilee followed and saw the tomb and how his body was laid" (Luke 23:55).

How do we see Jesus through these women's eyes as he is buried? We see the one who brought life to Jairus's daughter, the widow of Nain's son, and Mary and Martha's brother now lying dead himself. We see the one who could call dead people out of their graves being laid in a grave. We see the one who ordered that the stone over Lazarus's tomb be rolled away now having a stone rolled over his own tomb. We see the one who claimed to Martha that he was the resurrection and the life now lying dead and cold. Still, the women stuck with him. The question is, who came back to Jesus's tomb that Sunday morning, and what exactly did they see?

WITNESSES OF THE RESURRECTION

All four Gospels tell us that early on the first day of the week, women go to Jesus's tomb, and all four Gospels say that Mary Magdalene was there. But each Gospel gives a somewhat different list of other names. Ehrman points to these various lists as evidence that the accounts contradict. "Who was it who went to the tomb?" he asks:

> Was it Mary alone (John 20:1)? Mary and another Mary (Matthew 28:1)? Mary Magdalene, Mary the mother of James, and Salome (Mark 16:1)? Or women who had accompanied Jesus from Galilee to Jerusalem—possibly Mary Magdalene, Joanna, Mary the mother of James, and "other women" (Luke 24:1; see 23:55)?[7]

At first glance, these discrepancies seem troubling. But as Bauckham explains, they are not:

> The divergences among the lists have often been taken as grounds for not taking them seriously as

7. Bart Ehrman, *Jesus Interrupted: Revealing The Hidden Contradictions In The Bible (And Why We Don't Know About Them)* (New York: Harper-Collins, 2009), 47.

naming eyewitnesses of the events [of Jesus's death, burial, and resurrection]. In fact, the opposite is the case: these divergences, properly understood, demonstrate the scrupulous *care* with which the Gospels present the women as witnesses.[8]

Bauckham argues that, far from being confused, the Gospel authors "were careful to name precisely the women who were well known to them as witnesses."[9] What's more, while Ehrman observes that John's Gospel names only Mary Magdalene, he fails in his summary to note that John's Gospel also makes clear that Mary Magdalene was *not* alone. When she reports back to Peter John, she speaks as a representative of a group: "They have taken the Lord out of the tomb, and we do not know where they have laid him" (John 20:2). Ehrman's critique on the basis of the different lists of names does not hold water. But what about the differences between each Gospel's account of what the women saw? Is this, as Ehrman claims, evidence that the accounts are not to be trusted? I don't think so.

The first challenge is posed by Mark's Gospel. Mark tells us that the women wonder who will move the heavy stone on Jesus's tomb for them. But when they arrive, they find their problem has been solved:

8.   Bauckham, *Jesus and the Eyewitnesses*, 49.
9.   Bauckham, *Jesus and the Eyewitnesses*, 51.

And looking up, they saw that the stone had been rolled back—it was very large. And entering the tomb, they saw a young man sitting on the right side, dressed in a white robe, and they were alarmed. And he said to them, "Do not be alarmed. You seek Jesus of Nazareth, who was crucified. He has risen; he is not here. See the place where they laid him. But go, tell his disciples and Peter that he is going before you to Galilee. There you will see him, just as he told you." And they went out and fled from the tomb, for trembling and astonishment had seized them, and they said nothing to anyone, for they were afraid. (Mark 16:4–8)

This is likely the original ending of Mark's Gospel. If you open a modern Bible, you'll find additional verses with a note that reads, "Some of the earliest manuscripts do not include 16:9–20." Rather than leaving us with a neatly tied bow, the first Gospel to be written down ends with something more like a frayed knot. But we cannot conclude from this that the resurrection was a claim made up later. Mark's alarming man in white says of Jesus of Nazareth, "He has risen; he is not here," and he promises the women that they will see Jesus again, just as he told them (vv. 6–7).

What about the women's reaction? Unlike the other Gospel authors, Mark tells us that the women "said nothing to anyone, for they were afraid" (v. 8). But Mark cannot mean that the women never told anyone, or this scene could not have been included in Mark's Gospel!

Indeed, this ending of Mark's Gospel itself is evidence that the women *did* tell Peter, as they had been instructed, and Peter made sure their testimony was included in the Gospel written for him by Mark. Bauckham argues that, when Mark tells us that the women "said nothing to anyone," he does not mean that they didn't follow the angel's instruction to tell Jesus's apostles, but that they didn't spread the news to people in general. What's more, Bauckham suggests that Mark is not portraying the women as cowardly, but as having precisely the right reaction to this extraordinary news.[10]

The reality of Jesus's resurrection is quite terrifying. It washes over us because we're used to the idea. But finding Jesus's empty tomb and being told he's risen from the dead should leave these women shaking in their sandals—just as when Jesus calmed a storm with his words and his disciples "were filled with great fear" and asked, "Who then is this, that even the wind and the sea obey him?" (Mark 4:41). The resurrection proves that Jesus conquered death and that he is God's everlasting, universal, all-victorious King. The women are right to be afraid!

What about the differences in the various Gospel accounts of what the women saw and heard? Luke's text is similar to Mark's. But instead of one man in white, Luke tells us that the women meet "two men . . . in dazzling apparel," who tell them that Jesus has risen, just as he promised (Luke 24:1–7). Is Luke contradicting Mark by saying there were two men rather than one? No. In his

10. Bauckham, *Gospel Women*, 290.

resurrection account, Mark focuses our attention on one man, who speaks to the women, just as John focuses our attention on Mary Magdalene, despite there clearly being other women in the group.[11] We do this kind of thing today. I recently emailed my pastor, Curtis, to ask if my best friend Rachel and I could record a podcast in the church building. Curtis knows both me and Rachel well. He said, "Of course!" When I saw him later that afternoon, he asked about the podcast and was surprised to find that Rachel and I had been interviewed in person by the podcast host, who was in town that day. I hadn't mentioned the host in my email—despite the fact that her presence was the whole reason for the recording happening—because that detail was not relevant to my request. Likewise, the Gospel authors often simplify a scene by leaving out figures who are not vital to their point.

The Gospel authors also leave out many seemingly significant events as they condense Jesus's life, death, and resurrection into books that take between 1.5 and 2.5 hours each to read. For instance, Matthew is the only Gospel author who records the setting of a guard on Jesus's tomb, and he fills in what happens right before the women arrive:

> Now after the Sabbath, toward the dawn of the first day of the week, Mary Magdalene and the other

11. It's typical of Mark to offer a more condensed account. For example, when Mark tells the story of Jesus healing a blind man named Bartimaeus, he only mentions the one blind man (Mark 10:46–52), while Matthew references two (Matt. 20:29–34).

Mary went to see the tomb. And behold, there was a great earthquake, for an angel of the Lord descended from heaven and came and rolled back the stone and sat on it. His appearance was like lightning, and his clothing white as snow. And for fear of him the guards trembled and became like dead men. But the angel said to the women, "Do not be afraid, for I know that you seek Jesus who was crucified. He is not here, for he has risen, as he said. Come, see the place where he lay. Then go quickly and tell his disciples that he has risen from the dead, and behold, he is going before you to Galilee; there you will see him. See, I have told you." So they departed quickly from the tomb with fear and great joy, and ran to tell his disciples. (Matt. 28:1–8)

Matthew identifies the terrifying figure who talks to the women as an angel of the Lord. But this doesn't mean he's added wings to the alarming man in white of Mark's account. In the Bible, while angels are almost always frightening, they are rarely described as having wings and they are sometimes confused for humans (see Gen. 18:2–19:22).

Unlike Mark and Luke, but like John, Matthew also reports on a direct encounter that the women have with Jesus himself:

And behold, Jesus met them and said, "Greetings!" And they came up and took hold of his feet and worshiped him. Then Jesus said to them, "Do not be afraid; go and tell my brothers to go to Galilee, and there they will see me." (Matt. 28:9–10)

We might wonder how Luke could have left this encounter out. But he includes other resurrection appearances that Matthew does not narrate (Luke 24:13–49). As we read the resurrection accounts in Matthew, Mark, and Luke, we see how the different Gospel authors make different decisions about how they select, summarize, and emphasize their material. If we think about it, we regularly do the same.

In early December, a package arrived at our house. It contained a book of photographs. My daughter Eliza asked me who had sent it. I said, "Grandma." Eliza pushed back, "Grandma didn't send it. It came from someone called Susan." I said, "Yes, I know. Grandma's friend Susan took the photos in the book and Grandma bought the book from Susan and asked her to send it to Daddy on Grandma's behalf." It took Eliza a hot minute to disentangle what was going on! My original claim that Grandma had sent the book was a simplified version of what had happened, highlighting what I saw as the most relevant information. But Eliza's claim that it was actually Susan who'd sent the photo book, not Grandma herself, was also true.

If the Gospel authors were answering Eliza's question, Mark would've cut to the chase like me: "Grandma sent the photo book to Daddy." Matthew might have told us more: "Grandma's friend Susan sent the photo book for Daddy." Luke might have elaborated even further,

"Grandma paid her friend Susan, who is a photographer, to send the photo book to Mummy, so that Mummy could wrap it up for Daddy for Christmas." John would likely just have said, "Your Daddy loves photography. Grandma loves your Daddy. This gift shows that love." Like snapshots of a priceless work of art from different angles, each Gospel author gives us a unique perspective, drawn from the eyewitness accounts to which they had access. As John explains toward the end of his Gospel, his aim isn't to be exhaustive but to be persuasive: "Now Jesus did many other signs in the presence of the disciples ... but these are written so that you may believe that Jesus is the Christ, the Son of God, and that by believing you may have life in his name" (John 20:30–31). So, what about John's resurrection account?

'I HAVE SEEN THE LORD'

As so often in the Gospels, John takes a different tack to Matthew, Mark, and Luke. To begin with, he focuses our attention on Mary Magdalene alone:

> Now on the first day of the week Mary Magdalene came to the tomb early, while it was still dark, and saw that the stone had been taken away from the tomb. So she ran and went to Simon Peter and the other disciple, the one whom Jesus loved, and said to them, "They have taken the Lord out of the tomb, and we do not know where they have laid him." So Peter went out with the other disciple, and they were

going toward the tomb. Both of them were running together, but the other disciple outran Peter and reached the tomb first. And stooping to look in, he saw the linen cloths lying there, but he did not go in. Then Simon Peter came, following him, and went into the tomb. He saw the linen cloths lying there, and the face cloth, which had been on Jesus' head, not lying with the linen cloths but folded up in a place by itself. Then the other disciple, who had reached the tomb first, also went in, and he saw and believed; for as yet they did not understand the Scripture, that he must rise from the dead. Then the disciples went back to their homes. (John 20:1–10)

At first, we might think that John is damping down the role the women played and drawing attention to Peter and himself. Luke had also mentioned Peter's visit to the tomb, after he heard the women's report (Luke 24:12). So, highlighting Peter's role was not without precedent. But as we read on in John, we find that he places even more emphasis on Mary Magdalene than the other Gospel authors do.

First, we see Mary's encounter with the angels: "Mary stood weeping outside the tomb, and as she wept she stooped to look into the tomb. And she saw two angels in white, sitting where the body of Jesus had lain, one at the head and one at the feet" (John 20:11–12). But rather than reporting the message the angels gave to the women, John records a question they ask Mary: "Woman, why are you weeping?" She replies, "They have taken away my

Lord, and I do not know where they have laid him" (v. 13). Mary is grieving and bewildered. Not only has her Lord been crucified, his corpse appears also to have been stolen away, so she can't tend to his body as she'd hoped.

How do we see Jesus through Mary Magdalene's eyes in this moment? We don't. But then she turns around.

> Having said this, [Mary] turned around and saw Jesus standing, but she did not know that it was Jesus. Jesus said to her, "Woman, why are you weeping? Whom are you seeking?" Supposing him to be the gardener, she said to him, "Sir, if you have carried him away, tell me where you have laid him, and I will take him away." Jesus said to her, "Mary." She turned and said to him in Aramaic, "Rabboni!" (which means Teacher). (vv. 14–16)

At the sound of her most common name, Mary's tear-filled eyes are opened, and she sees the risen Lord for who he is. Mary responds with one of the few Aramaic words in John's Gospel: "Rabboni!"—a variant form of rabbi. She hails the risen Jesus with a word that speaks to her discipleship. Indeed, this weeping woman is the disciple to whom the resurrected Jesus first reveals himself.

Matthew records that Mary Magdalene and the other Mary took hold of Jesus's feet and worshiped him (Matt. 28:9). So, we should likely imagine Mary Magdalene clinging to his feet when Jesus sends her on a mission:

Jesus said to her, "Do not cling to me, for I have not
yet ascended to the Father; but go to my brothers
and say to them, 'I am ascending to my Father and
your Father, to my God and your God.'" Mary Magdalene went and announced to the disciples, "I have
seen the Lord"—and that he had said these things to
her. (John 20:17–18)

In a culture where women were often silenced, Jesus
commissions a female disciple to announce his resurrection to his male disciples. Strikingly, Mary Magdalene is
the first person in John's Gospel to call Jesus "the Lord."[12]
The expression has been used three times to refer to Israel's covenant God (John 1:23; 12:13, 38) and twice by
the author of John to refer to Jesus (John 6:23; 11:2). But
now, in this moment of revelation, Mary tells the other
disciples, "I have seen the Lord."

WOMEN AS EYEWITNESSES

"I'll believe it when I see it" is one of my husband's favorite lines. He's a born-again follower of Jesus, but in
other respects, a natural skeptic. Like Bryan, historians
in Jesus's day placed a high value on seeing: "I'll believe
it if you saw it" would have been a fitting motto for their
guild. With this no doubt in mind, the Gospel authors

---

12. Jesus is addressed as "Lord" by multiple other people in John's Gospel
before this point (e.g. John 6:68; 8:11; 9:38; 11:3, 12, 21, 27, 32, 39; 13:6, 9, 25,
36, 37; 14:5, 8), but he is not referred to as "the Lord."

repeatedly make the women in their final chapters the subjects of seeing verbs. As Bauckham notes,

> [The women] "saw" the events as Jesus died (Matt 27:55; Mark 15:40; Luke 23:49), they "saw" where he was laid in the tomb (Mark 15:47; Luke 23:55), they went on the first day of the week to "see" the tomb (Matt 28:1), they "saw" the stone rolled away (Mark 16:4), they "saw" the young man sitting on the right side (Mark 16:5), and the angel invited them to "see" the empty place where Jesus' body had lain (Matt 28:6; Mark 16:6).

"It could hardly be clearer," Bauckham concludes, "that the Gospels are appealing to their role as eyewitnesses."[13] In light of this, Mary Magdalene's announcement, "I have seen the Lord," is doubly significant. Like a modern day journalist with photo footage to back up her story, she's standing as an eyewitness of Jesus's resurrection, not only to the apostles, but also to the reader.

The fact that all four Gospels make the women central to their resurrection claim appeals to us as 21st-century readers. But it would have had the opposite effect on literate men in the Greco-Roman world. As Bauckham explains, "women were thought by educated men to be gullible in religious matters and especially prone to superstitious fantasy and excessive religious practices."[14]

13. Bauckham, *Jesus and the Eyewitnesses*, 48.
14. Bauckham, *Gospel Women*, 270.

The second-century Greek philosopher Celsus was voicing what many of his contemporaries would've thought when he took aim at Mary Magdalene:

> After death [Jesus] rose again and showed the marks of his punishment and how his hands had been pierced. But who saw this? A hysterical female, as you say, and perhaps some other one of those who were deluded by the same sorcery.[15]

From Celsus's perspective, Mary Magdalene and the other weeping women who witnessed Jesus's so-called resurrection were a joke. If the Gospel authors had been making up their stories, they could have made Joseph of Arimathea and Nicodemus the first resurrection witnesses: two well-respected men involved in Jesus's burial. The only possible reason for the emphasis on the testimony of women—and weeping women at that—is if they really *were* the witnesses.

At first, even Jesus's apostles were skeptical. Luke tells us, "it was Mary Magdalene and Joanna and Mary the mother of James and the other women with them who told these things to the apostles, but these words seemed to them an idle tale, and they did not believe them" (Luke 24:10–11). These women had traveled with Jesus throughout his ministry. They should have been trusted by his male disciples. But as usual, the Gospel authors faithfully preserve the apostles' most mortifying

15. Origen, *Contra Celsum*, 2:55, quoted in Bauckham, *Gospel Women*, 271.

failures: from Peter's denial that he even knew Jesus to Thomas's refusal to believe that he had risen from the dead unless he saw it with his own eyes (John 20:24–29). Again, if the Gospel authors had felt free to fabricate, they surely would not have dreamed up this embarrassing portrayal of key leaders in the early church. But the apostles seem to have embraced these humbling records of their great mistakes, as they threw light on the great triumph of their Savior.

Like the film *Red Notice*, the story of the Gospels depends on a claim about something that happened 2,000 years ago. The premise of *Red Notice* is a fake. As far as anybody knows, Mark Antony did not give Cleopatra three bejeweled eggs. The movie is a fun-filled fiction from its beginning to its sequel-setup end. But the Gospel accounts of Jesus's death, burial, and resurrection are the opposite of fake. Indeed, they fail to fit the script of what first-century authors would have made up in a host of ways. They offer us a crucified Messiah, whose resurrection was first seen by weeping women, and the more we understand of how biographies were written in that time and place, the clearer it becomes that the Gospel authors are presenting us with life-changing, authentic, unexpected eyewitness testimony. We may choose not to believe it. But unlike the fake egg in the museum scene, the women's claim that they saw Jesus crucified, entombed, and raised to life on the third day does not disintegrate when tested. And if it's true, it's far more valuable than any ancient artifact. It is the very source of life itself.

DISCUSSION QUESTIONS

Getting Started: What is something you've witnessed that you might not believe if you hadn't seen it yourself?

1. How does Jesus care for his mother as he is dying on the cross?

2. Who were the women who witnessed Jesus's crucifixion? What do we know about them?

3. What do you know about Mary Magdalene from previous chapters? How does this knowledge enrich your understanding of her interaction with the risen Christ?

4. Why is it unconventional for the eyewitnesses of Jesus's resurrection to be women? What does their inclusion reveal about Jesus's attitude toward them?

5. Read John 10:27–28. In light of these verses, how is Mary Magdalene's interaction with the risen Christ a picture of our salvation?

6. What situation in your life feels hopeless? How does seeing the death, burial, and resurrection of Christ through these women's eyes give you hope in your devastation?

7. When Mary Magdalene saw the risen Christ, she acknowledged him as "the Lord." As you see the risen Christ through her eyes, who do you say that he is? Have you acknowledged Jesus as the Lord?

8. How do you see Jesus most meaningfully through the eyes of these women?

Going Deeper: Read John 20:1–18.

1. How many times does the passage refer to Mary weeping? How does the passage emphasize her grief turning to joy? In what way is this transition a picture of the Christian life?

2. After seeing the risen Christ, Mary declares that she has "seen the Lord." How do verses 9 and 16 inform our understanding of someone's ability to see Jesus rightly?

3. How does Jesus affirm women as disciples of Jesus and reliable eyewitnesses in verse 17?

CONCLUSION

THE GOSPELS OF
THE MARYS

IN THE SO-CALLED Gospel of Mary with which this
book began, Peter asks Mary to share her revelation from
the Lord. Mary agrees. Much of the text at this point
is lost, but what remains communicates an esoteric dialogue about the soul. When Mary has finished, Andrew
responds, "Say what you will about the things she has
said, but I do not believe that the Savior said these things,
for indeed these teachings are strange ideas." We see his
point. Jesus in Mary's revelation sounds almost nothing
like the Jesus of the Gospels. Peter, by contrast, grounds
his objection in Mary's sex: "Did he, then, speak with
a woman in private without our knowing about it? Are
we to turn around and listen to her? Did he choose her

over us?"[1] In this depiction of Peter, we see all the possibilities of anti-female bias. But as we have seen in the course of this book, we don't need the Gospel of Mary to counteract this prejudice. This fictional Peter's misogyny withers in the light of the Gospels of Matthew, Mark, Luke, and John.

The Gospel of Mary's Peter objects that Jesus would not have spoken with a woman in private without the male apostles knowing it. But as we saw in chapter 3, Jesus had his longest private conversation with a Samaritan woman, while his male disciples were elsewhere. In response to Mary's testimony, the Gospel of Mary's Peter complains, "Are we to turn around and listen to her?" But as we saw in chapter 6, all four New Testament Gospels show Mary Magdalene being commissioned to tell the apostles that Jesus had risen from the dead. The Gospel of Mary's Peter complains, "Did he choose her over us?" But Matthew and John both show us the risen Jesus meeting with Mary Magdalene. In John's Gospel in particular, it's clear that Jesus could have met with Peter first, when Peter came running to the empty tomb. But Jesus chose to meet with Mary Magdalene instead, and for her and the other women to pass on the news of his resurrection to Peter and the rest of the apostles. Rather than her revelation being a mystical dialogue about the soul, however, Mary Magdalene reported on a concrete, flesh-and-blood encounter with her resurrected Lord.

1. Quoted from Karen L. King's translation in King, *Gospel of Mary Magdala*, 15–17.

To look at Jesus through the eyes of women may seem at first like an innately modern project. But when it comes to Jesus's death and resurrection, it's precisely what the Gospel authors invite us to do. What we see through their eyes is not an alternative Jesus, but rather the authentic Jesus, who welcomes both men and women as his disciples, and who is best seen from below. The women who brought their sin and shame and desperate need and threw themselves at Jesus's feet reveal how Jesus treated those who were despised by others. The women who sat at Jesus's feet to learn from him help us to recognize our teacher, who brings words of everlasting life. The women who grasped hold of Jesus's feet when they first saw him risen from the dead help us to see that Jesus is the Lord of heaven and earth even today.

The testimony of women is not just tacked on to the end of the Gospels. It's also woven in. I noted in the introduction that if we worked through Matthew, Mark, Luke, and John and cut out all the scenes that were *not* witnessed by women, we'd only lose a small proportion of the texts. But even if we limited our scope still further and only kept the parts of Jesus's life that were witnessed by women named Mary, we'd lose very little! Indeed, we could legitimately call the Bible's four accounts of Jesus's life the Gospels of the Marys, as they've preserved for us the testimony of at least five—Jesus's mother, Mary Magdalene, Mary of Bethany, Mary the wife of Clopas, and Mary the mother of James and Joseph—whose knowledge of Jesus stretched from his conception to his resurrection.

The Gospels in our Bibles are the Gospels of the women Jesus loved. Each one bears female fingerprints. Matthew and Luke are the Gospels of Mary the mother of Jesus, who first found out that Jesus is the Son of God and that he'd be the everlasting King. Matthew is the Gospel of the mother of the sons of Zebedee, who followed Jesus to his crucifixion, where she saw him prove his claim that he would give his life as a ransom for many. Matthew and Mark are the Gospels of Mary the mother of James and Joseph, who witnessed Jesus's death and burial and resurrection, and of the Gentile woman whose humble faith led to her daughter being healed. Mark is the Gospel of Salome, who'd been with Jesus since the early days in Galilee and witnessed him both crucified and raised. Matthew, Mark, and Luke are the Gospels of Peter's mother-in-law, who served as soon as she was healed; of the woman who had bled for 12 long years, but told herself, "If only I can touch the hem of his garment, I will be made whole"; and of the 12-year-old girl, whom Jesus raised from death as easily as if he'd woken her from sleep.

I called my own son Luke because Luke's Gospel bears so many unique female fingerprints. It's not only the Gospel that gives us Mary's testimony about Jesus's conception and her incredible song of praise to God, but it's also the Gospel of Elizabeth, who recognized the embryonic Jesus as her Lord, and of Anna, who prophesied that the infant Jesus had come to redeem Israel. It's the Gospel of Martha of Bethany, who welcomed Jesus into her home, and of Mary of Bethany, who sat at Jesus's feet and learned from him. It's the Gospel of Joanna, the wife of Chuza, who left Herod's court to follow Jesus all the way to the empty tomb, and of Susanna, whose story has been lost to us, but who was sufficiently well known to Luke's first readers that she needed no other introduction. What's more, Luke is the Gospel of many unnamed women Jesus helped and dignified—like the sinful woman of the city, the widow of Nain, and the disabled woman in the synagogue.

John is the Gospel of multiple women whose stories we would not have known from any other source—like the Samaritan woman at the well, who drank the living water and proclaimed to her hometown that Jesus is the Christ, and Mary the wife of Clopas, who saw her nephew nailed to a cross. But it's also the Gospel that carries on the stories of some women we have met in other Gospels. In John, Martha of Bethany finds that Jesus is the resurrection and the life, and Mary of Bethany is named as the woman who poured ointment on his feet. And poignantly, in John, Mary the mother of Jesus not only witnesses her son turn water into wine, but also watches as his life is poured out on the cross. Indeed, in John we see that Jesus forged a special bond between its author and his mother from the cross. Finally, in John we see Mary Magdalene, from whom Luke tells us Jesus cast out seven demons—and to whose presence at the cross and empty tomb all the four Gospels testify—become the person to whom Jesus speaks his first post-resurrection words.

How do we see Jesus through these women's eyes? We see him as the one who heals our hurts and meets our needs. We see him as the one who takes our sin upon himself and welcomes us with unimaginable love. We see him as the one who sees *us*, even when all others turn away, and as the one who welcomes us to learn from him and pour our meager love out at his feet. We see him as the one who is the Savior of the world and yet knows us each by name—even if we answer to the most common name in town. We see him as the one who gathers up our broken hearts and bodies in his arms, and as the only one who has the power to make us whole. We see him as the one who faced the horror of God's judgment on the cross, so he could turn his face to us and call us into everlasting life.

Mary of Nazareth was the first to hear about Jesus, before he was ever born from her womb. Mary of Magdalene was the first to see him after he was reborn from the tomb. Some have claimed that the second-century document now known as the Gospel of Mary records her most authentic testimony. Really, Mary's most authentic message comes to us through the first-century document known as the Gospel of John, and it is this: "I have seen the Lord" (John 20:18).

Let's look at Jesus through her eyes today. No vision is more beautiful.

DISCUSSION QUESTIONS

1. How has your perspective on the New Testament Gospels evolved through reading this book?

2. What five words would you use to describe Jesus in light of what you've read?
3. What have you learned about yourself as a result of seeing Jesus through the eyes of women?
4. How should you move forward differently in light of this new understanding?
5. How does glimpsing Jesus through these eyewitnesses compel you to worship?

ACKNOWLEDGMENTS

I DON'T HAVE a ghostwriter. But I do have multiple ghost readers, and this is my chance to bring them out of the shadows and say thank you.

Right before Christmas 2021, I sent an early draft to two very different friends—Christine Caine and Rachel Gilson. As usual when I write a book and no one else has seen it, I thought it was probably terrible. Christine read it between December 23 and 25 and sent me invaluable, blow-by-blow feedback via text. Rachel didn't even tell me she was reading it until she'd finished and then sent me all her feedback at once, with the inimitable note: "I didn't tell you I was reading it because I didn't want you to hassle me!" I'm thankful for both their sets of eyes. They looked from slightly different angles and made this thoroughly imperfect book much better than it would have been.

My second set of ghost readers was Julia Rosenbloom and Paige Brooks. Julia gave me useful feedback from her Jewish perspective, and Paige helped me see how it would land with a growing Christian who is relatively new to reading the Bible. Both these friends gulped it down in record time because they knew I needed feedback soon. I'm deeply thankful for their time and help.

My third set of eyes was far more expert than my own. Nathan Riddlehoover and Christopher Cowan both have PhDs in New Testament, and they sent me many important corrections. Any remaining errors are my own, but there would have been far more without their input!

Ivan Mesa, Joanna Kimbrel, and Cassie Watson were this book's formal editors. Their careful work caught various mistakes and prompted multiple improvements. I'm grateful to them and to Joanna in particular for writing the discussion questions that accompany this book.

I'm thankful to Julius Kim and Collin Hansen from The Gospel Coalition for once again letting me write a book at breakneck speed; and to my husband, Bryan; and to my children, Miranda, Eliza, and Luke, for their unstinting love and support.

For me, at least, it takes a village of love to write a book. I'm thankful for my village.

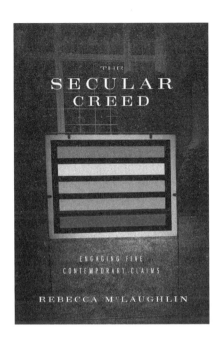

"Rebecca McLaughlin offers a gentle, yet powerful biblical corrective that calls readers to holistic Christian love—a higher calling than the call of the culture, and, often, a harder calling. She examines popular cultural mantras and answers each one with the truth and application of the gospel of Christ. In her balanced and gracious approach, she paints our culture's arguments in the most compassionate light possible—and then shows the beauty of a more excellent way!"

—JASMINE HOLMES, *author of* Mother to Son: Letters to a Black Boy on Identity and Hope

In *Confronting Jesus*, Rebecca McLaughlin shares important biblical context to help all readers see why the Gospels should be taken seriously as historical documents. Exploring eyewitness testimony about Jesus, McLaughlin points to him as a first-century Jewish man who is the Son of God, King of the Jews, mighty healer, greatest teacher, lover of sinners, suffering servant, perfect sacrifice, and universal Lord. This follow-up to her first book, *Confronting Christianity*, helps readers understand the message of the Gospels and explore who Jesus really is.

10 Questions Every Teen Should Ask (and Answer) about Christianity

REBECCA McLAUGHLIN

"Young people might not always articulate their questions about life. But they are wondering. *10 Questions Every Teen Should Ask (and Answer) about Christianity* can help them both express and satisfy their emerging questions and longings. We wish we'd had this book when we were raising our children! But now we can give it away—confidently—starting with our own grandchildren."

—RAY AND JANI ORTLUND, *President and Executive Vice President, Renewal Ministries*

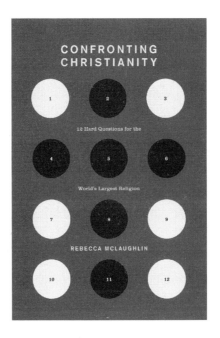

CONFRONTING
CHRISTIANITY

12 Hard Questions for the

World's Largest Religion

REBECCA MCLAUGHLIN

"This book is compelling reading, not only because of its intellectual rigor and the fact that it is beautifully written but also because of its honest, empathetic humanity. Readers will find themselves expertly guided on a journey that involves them not only in confronting Christianity but also in confronting themselves—their worldviews, hopes, fears, failures, and search for identity and satisfaction—and, finally, in confronting Christ as the altogether credible source of life as God means it to be."

—JOHN C. LENNOX, *Emeritus Professor of Mathematics, University of Oxford*

TGC THE GOSPEL COALITION

THE GOSPEL COALITION (TGC) supports the church in making disciples of all nations, by providing gospel-centered resources that are trusted and timely, winsome and wise.

Guided by a Council of more than 40 pastors in the Reformed tradition, TGC seeks to advance gospel-centered ministry for the next generation by producing content (including articles, podcasts, videos, courses, and books) and convening leaders (including conferences, virtual events, training, and regional chapters).

In all of this we want to help Christians around the world better grasp the gospel of Jesus Christ and apply it to all of life in the 21st century. We want to offer biblical truth in an era of great confusion. We want to offer gospel-centered hope for the searching.

Join us by visiting TGC.org so you can be equipped to love God with all your heart, soul, mind, and strength, and to love your neighbor as yourself.